THE HISTORY OF JESUS:
THE BIBLE IN A NUTSHELL

William Davis

ISBN 978-1-63784-281-2 (paperback)
ISBN 978-1-63784-283-6 (hardcover)
ISBN 978-1-63784-282-9 (digital)

Hawes & Jenkins Publishing
16427 N Scottsdale Road Suite 410
Scottsdale, AZ 85254
www.hawesjenkins.com

Printed in the United States of America

ACKNOWLEDGMENTS

I may know more about the Bible than anything else, but that does not make me an expert. I love the Bible and its message of hope and salvation. My fellow Christian brother and member of First United Methodist Church in Denham Springs, Louisiana, Bob Hill, was a tremendous help to me in ensuring the accuracy of the manuscript and correcting bad syntax. Ms. Colleen O'Connor, a retired English and literature teacher, helped me by reminding me that I needed to stay on theme and making hundreds of punctuation corrections. My son, Daniel, ripped apart my work and got me onto a new track that turned out to be this summary of the Bible that I hope will encourage people to dig deep into God's Word and find out what God's message and will for their lives are. Steve Doan, my fellow officer of the artillery in Vietnam and now a retired army chaplain, gave me great encouragement.

Book cover image: Painting by Pacino da Bonaguida, circa 1310, The Tree of Life," Academia Museum, Florence, Italy.

INTRODUCTION

The Bible is, for many people, the most exciting book ever written. It may be the most important book ever written, yet it is also one of the most difficult to understand. It is fundamentally a book of love—God's love letter to us. However, it contains much violence, evil, and intrigue. And what is more, many of the stories of the Bible reveal questionable, if not evil, character traits, even among direct ancestors of Jesus.

If you are one of the many people who do not read the Bible because it is difficult and confusing, I want to simplify it for you so that it becomes your guide for daily living. My purpose in writing this book is to help you make sense of the Bible and know that there are lessons in every one of its sixty-six books from God to you. God gave us his Word to change our character so we can become more like His son, Jesus, who was His gift of love to us.

The order in which the books of the Bible occur is one of the keys to understanding it. Obviously, the Bible is divided into two sections: the Old and New Testaments. Since the Bible is all about the coming of the Messiah, Jesus Christ, in the Old Testament, and the life of Jesus Christ and establishment of His church in the New Testament, the most significant ordering is the organization of the Old Testament. Most scholars say that the books are grouped by literary type or genre—law, history, poetry, and prophecy—and I agree that they are grouped as such. But I do not believe that this grouping by genre helps us understand the Bible nearly as well as studying it from a genealogical view. As to prophecy, we will find that there are prophecies in nearly all the Old Testament books.

The Bible has existed in some form or other for a few thousand years, dating back to when, according to tradition, Moses, some 3,400 years ago, wrote Genesis, Exodus, Leviticus, Deuteronomy, and Numbers. These five books were referred to in Jewish lexicon as the Pentateuch and were also known as the Torah, or the books of the law.

What is so important about the Pentateuch? It reveals the earliest written history of man from the creation of Adam and Eve, the first man and woman, the great flood, which wiped out all of mankind, except for Noah's family, to the repopulation of the earth with all the diverse characters that lived in and around the fertile crescent and were fundamental in carrying out God's purposes in creating a people that He called His own. The Pentateuch contains the Ten Commandments, those laws which God gave to Moses on Mount Sinai after the children of Israel escaped from approximately four hundred years of enslavement to the Egyptians. These laws stipulated the way people were to live, both in relation to God and to each other, and they are as applicable to us today as they were to the Israelites over three thousand years ago. In fact, they are the basis for the Judeo-Christian tenets upon which the laws of the Christian nations of the world are based.

All well and good you say, but there is so much in the Bible that begs the question, "Why is that particular story or account in the Bible?" We understand the places of Abraham, Jacob, and Joseph in the history of the Christian religion, more specifically the Jewish religion. We know about King Solomon, the son of David, who was supposedly the wisest man who ever lived. Solomon and David are prominent in the ancestry of Jesus. We know who Jesus's disciples were, who the Apostle Paul was, and the role Paul played in establishing the first Christian churches in what we know now as the Middle East. But what about such characters as Judah, Rahab the Harlot, Samson, Boaz, Ruth, and Jesse? Who was Gideon, and why did God choose him, a man with no battle experience, for a mission of war against people who had conquered a tribe of the Jews and were treating them badly? Why did one of the prophets of the Old Testament knowingly marry a prostitute?

These are very legitimate and even perplexing questions, which I hope to explain so that you will understand the complete story of the Bible, including many diverse people who are critical to an understanding of who Jesus really is. You will understand why Jesus is God incarnate, not just an angel or prophet. Many of these characters in the Old Testament, both good and bad, are listed in the genealogies in the books of Matthew and Luke as direct ancestors of Jesus Christ.

This is not an in-depth scholarly work, but a simple expository meant to whet your appetite to go deeper into God's Word and enjoy its message to you.

The chronology of the Bible, the order in which it was written, generally coincides with the genealogy of Jesus; therefore, giving us the complete history of Jesus from Adam and Eve to His death and resurrection and the establishment of His church by His apostles in the New Testament. The genealogical thread runs throughout the Old Testament all the way to Jesus's birth in the New Testament.

The genealogy of Jesus Christ in the first chapter of the gospel of Matthew begins with Abraham who begat Isaac all the way through Joseph, the husband of Mary of whom was born Jesus who is called Christ. The book of Luke contains the genealogy of Jesus in reverse order from Mary, the mother of Jesus, back to Adam and Eve. Note that Matthew's account of Jesus's genealogy shows that Joseph came through Solomon, David's son from Bathsheba, and Luke's account of Jesus's genealogy shows Mary came through Nathan, one of David's other sons (2 Samuel 5:14). This lineage shows Jesus's ancestry dating back to Adam and Eve, the original parents God created to begin the process of populating the earth.

Genesis begins with Adam, and although it tells of many other ancestors or key figures, it tells the story of Adam's descendants in their genealogical order. It is important to note that many of these people are revealed as "types of Christ." A type of Christ is a person who, by their actions, led to the saving or freeing of other people from some kind of bondage, capture, or enslavement.

I will touch on several actions or incidents which, even by today's standards, could be considered "unholy." In this book, I will explain or describe how God uses all kinds of people for His purposes. God uses these people to demonstrate that He is a Holy God, a jealous God, a God of Love, a God of forgiveness, and a God whose mercies are new every morning as the prophet Jeremiah says in the Bible book, *The Lamentations of Jeremiah*, more concisely known as *Lamentations* (chapter 3:22–23). "*The Lord's lovingkindnesses never cease, for His compassions never fail. They are new every morning; great is thy faithfulness.*" When the children of Israel, God's chosen people, would go astray or suffer hardship because of their disobedience, God would use certain people to get their attention and say, "Return to me. Return to your first love. I have not divorced you. You have divorced me, and I want you back."

Isn't it a wonderful thing that His mercies are new every morning? That means that when we sin, we can bow before God and say, "Father, I have sinned. I am sorry for my sin and ask that you forgive me." God then extends his mercy to us and forgives and restores our relationship with Him. God wants us to strive to live a life free of sin, but He knows that He created humans who are going to sin because He gave us free will. That is why He gave His Son, Jesus, to be the propitiation for our sin. In other words, Jesus would atone for our sins and pay the penalty for us by dying on the cross.

Why? God wants us to know that no matter what kind of despicable actions we may commit, we have an advocate in Jesus Christ, who even though perfect in every way, was born of sinful ancestors. He was born of the Virgin Mary, so He was God Incarnate. Jesus was the son of God sent to earth to be a human just as we are, except without sin. Jesus came to earth to show us how we are to live in relation to each other and in relation to God. Mary's father and the father of Joseph, her husband, were in the lineage of Jesus, which Luke extends all the way back to the creation of Adam and Eve. Jesus was the son of God, sent to earth to be born of a virgin. This is the meaning of being incarnate, being made of flesh, a human being.

I have written this book in two parts: the Old Testament and the New Testament. "Part 1: The Old Testament" begins with the creation of man, which leads to the early history of the Jewish people beginning with Abraham. It is Abraham's descendants who are God's chosen people. The people and events in the Old Testament point to the coming of a Messiah for the oft-conquered Hebrews, mainly due to their disobedience to God. This Messiah was Jesus.

In "Part 2: The New Testament," I explain the account of the foretold Messiah, beginning with His birth and life on earth, His teachings, His death on a cross for our sins, and His resurrection. After His ascension to heaven, His apostles carried out his command to make disciples of all nations and establish His church. Paul's letters, which are called epistles, to the churches he established throughout Asia Minor, are summarized for you in part 2 of this book.

This is a layman's explanation of each book to entice you to get into the Bible's pages and make your own discoveries from this great gift from God, the story of Jesus. It is written simply, straightforward, and short. It is good to be a Bible scholar, but this book will not accomplish that. My goal is to whet your appetite and get you to read the Bible and let God reveal it to you.

I have used the New American Standard Bible as my biblical reference. Any biblical quotes I use are taken from the NASB. I found its language easy to read and understand.

PART I

THE OLD TESTAMENT

CHAPTER I

GENESIS

In Genesis, the first book of the Bible, we see several examples of types of Christ, notably Noah, Abraham, Isaac, Joseph, and Moses. These men were used by God specifically to exemplify the character of Jesus as a savior to His people. We start out with the creation story.

In the beginning, the first day, God created the heaven and the earth. On the sixth day, he created a man, whom he named Adam. He placed Adam in the Garden of Eden to cultivate and keep it. The Lord God told Adam that *"from any tree of the garden you may eat freely, but from the tree of the knowledge of good and evil you shall not eat, for in the day that you eat from it, you shall surely die"* (Genesis 2:16–17). This is the first of seven covenants that God made with men in the Old Testament. This covenant, called the Edenic Covenant, was an agreement that Adam would populate the earth, subdue the earth, exercise dominion over the animal creation, care for the Garden of Eden and enjoy its fruit, and refrain from eating the fruit of the tree of the knowledge of good and evil under punishment of death. After some time passed, God decided it was not good for Adam to be alone, so He created Eve to be his companion.

God created Adam and Eve perfect and gave them the ability to think and reason; that is, He gave them "free will." Unfortunately, there existed an evil being, whom we know as Satan. Satan was a fallen angel, who God had kicked out of heaven and to whom God gave dominion over the earth. Satan, being crafty, took the form of a serpent and apparently was a comely being. This serpent was determined to cause Adam and Eve to fall under his control. One day, he said to Eve, "*Indeed, has God said, 'You shall not eat from any tree of the garden?*'" Eve responded that God said that they could eat of any tree, except the one in the middle of the garden; and if they ate from that tree, they would die. The serpent said to Eve, "*You surely shall not die. For God knows that in the day you eat from it your eyes will be opened, and you shall be like God, knowing good and evil*" (Genesis 3:1–5).

That sounded reasonable to Eve, so seeing that the tree was good for food, a delight to the eyes, and desirable to make one wise, she took from its fruit and ate. Then she gave also to Adam, and he ate with her. The Bible says that the eyes of both were opened, and they knew that they were naked. So they sewed fig leaves together and made themselves loin coverings.

Genesis then says that God came walking in the garden, and Adam and Eve hid themselves from God. God called out for them, and Adam said he was afraid to answer because he was naked. God asked how he knew that he was naked and asked if they had eaten from the forbidden tree, which God had commanded them to avoid.

Adam did what people do when they are caught in a wrong; he blamed someone else; that someone, of course, being Eve. Eve, in turn, blamed the serpent.

This disobedience ended the Edenic Covenant. God then told them the consequences of their disobedience. God placed a curse on the serpent and said he would crawl on his belly and eat dust forever. *To the serpent he said, "I will put enmity between you and the woman and between your seed and her seed; he shall bruise you on the head and you shall bruise him on the heel." To Eve he said, "I will greatly multiply your pain in childbirth, in pain you shall bring forth children; yet your desire shall be for your husband, and he shall rule over you"* (Genesis 3:15–16). This is the second general covenant between God and man and is called the Adamic Covenant.

Let us look at this covenant in more detail. First, the serpent, the instrument used by Satan to trick Eve and consequently Adam, is cursed by God. The curse affects both the serpent and Satan. Great physical changes took place in the serpent. Apparently, the serpent walked upright but now has to crawl on its belly. It was previously the most desirable animal of the animal creation; now it is the most loathsome. The sight or thought of a snake to most people should be an effective reminder of the devastating effects of sin. Second, in Genesis 3:15, Satan is judged; and third, we see the first prophecy of Jesus told. The bruising of the heel is the foretelling of Jesus's ordeal on the cross, and the crushing of the serpent's head foretells Jesus's victory over Satan when He would rise from the dead, showing that Satan has no power at all over Jesus and no power over us when we have put our faith and trust in Jesus Christ. The rest of the covenant indicates that death was introduced into the human race, creating the need for Adam and Eve to procreate. Eve is told there will be pain in childbirth, and that she is made subject to her husband. The ground is cursed and is to bring forth weeds among the food, which man must eat for his existence.

> Then the Lord God said, "Behold, the man has become like one of Us, knowing good and evil, and now, lest he stretch out his hand and take also from the tree of life, and eat, and live forever" therefore, God sent them out

from the garden of Eden to cultivate
the ground from which he was taken."
(Genesis 3:22–23)

Some of the important early characters in Genesis
are enumerated following Adam's and Eve's expulsion
from the Garden of Eden, starting with Cain and Abel.
Cain killed his brother, Abel, because he was jealous
that Abel had offered a more acceptable sacrifice to
God than he had. God cursed Cain so that his produce
from the ground was greatly reduced, and he became a
wanderer. Cain then settled in the land of Nod, east of
Eden. Jealousy was the first sin mentioned in the Bible,
and that jealousy led to murder. Jealousy is a dangerous
thing. Proverbs 27:4 says that jealousy is more dangerous than anger or wrath.

Genesis then enumerates the generations following Cain, and we discover that men lived very long
lives, most notably Methuselah, who lived to be 969
years old. God was sad that he had created mankind
who was destined to be evil. God said, "I will destroy
the world by a great flood, yet I will not destroy Noah
because I have found him to be righteous." If you do
the math, you find that Methuselah was still living at
the time of the great flood when all the inhabitants of
the earth drowned with the exception of Noah and his
family and two of every kind of animal that existed
at that time. They, of course, were safely born by the

ark that God commanded Noah to build to save them from the coming flood. And if Methuselah were alive, then assuredly so were his children and his grandchildren. So we see that God's judgment is quite severe, in that everyone except Noah and his wife and Noah's two sons and their wives perished in the flood. We know that Noah lived to be quite old as well because it took him 120 years to build the ark. Genesis 7:11 says that Noah was 599 years old (in his 600th year) when the rains that flooded the earth began. We see then that Noah and his following generations contain the direct ancestors of Jesus.

Ten generations after Noah, we come to perhaps the most important character in Jesus's lineage and the beginning of the tribes of Israel and the Jewish faith. This person was Abraham, the patriarch of the Jewish nation. Abraham was at the time called Abram (exalted father), and he first comes on the scene in a place called Ur of the Chaldees, which for point of reference, would be in present-day Iraq. Ur, in the province of Haran, was about five hundred miles east of present-day Israel, known in early Biblical times as the Land of Canaan. God told Abram to leave the area in which he was living, to leave his relatives and travel to a land He would show him, and that He would make of him a great nation.

Right away, we see faith at work. God spoke to Abram. Was it an audible voice, an angel, or was it a dream? We are not told other than God told Abram to go, and in faith, Abram obeyed. Abram was seventy-five years old when he left Haran, and he took with him his wife, Sarai, all their possessions, and his nephew, Lot. Sarai was ten years younger than Abram.

The apostle Paul in Romans chapter 4 says that Abram's faith was counted to him as righteousness because he continued to be obedient to and trust God. What a wonderful statement. When we have faith in God and obey him, then we too can be called righteous. But that is a very high calling. How can we be righteous if we are all sinners? In Isaiah 64:6, we read that *"all our righteousness are as filthy rags before God."* The answer is in 2 Corinthians 5:21, Jesus has paid our debt of sin, and we become the righteousness of God in Christ when we accept his death on the cross for our salvation. After that, we are to strive to live in obedience to God; and when we sin, we can confess that sin to God and be made whole again.

Abram and Lot came into the land of Canaan looking for a fertile place for their livestock and settled west of the Jordan River. However, they continued to move about the land, always hunting for greener pastures for their flocks. During one particular time of famine, they moved down to Egypt. Sarai was a very beautiful woman even at her age, and Abram was afraid pharaoh would kill him and take Sarai from him, so he told Sarai to say that she was his sister. Pharaoh took notice of Sarai and decided he wanted her for his harem, and he sent and took her from Abram. He gave Abram livestock, gold, and servants. God brought plagues on pharaoh and told him in a dream that he would die because he had taken Abram's wife. Pharaoh quickly returned Sarai to Abram and told Abram to leave Egypt. So Abram migrated back north into the Land of Canaan. Did Abram lie to pharaoh that Sarai was his sister? Sarai was Abram's half-sister. They had the same father but different mothers. Why did Abram tell this half-truth? He was human. He feared for his life, but it appears that, in the heat of the moment as it were, he might have temporarily forgotten God's promise to make of him a great nation.

God had promised Abram he would make of him a great nation. But that would require Abram and his wife, Sarai, to have children. However, the Bible indicates that when Abram was eighty-six years old and his wife was ten years younger, they still had no children. Childbearing age for Sarai assuredly was past. But Abram kept the faith. He trusted that God, who said He would make of Abram a great nation, would make it come to pass.

Sarai apparently did not have as much faith as her husband. After being the obedient wife and following Abram for all these years, she decided to "help God out." She devised the plan of letting Abram father a child by their Egyptian handmaiden, Hagar. Was that

God's plan? Probably not. How did that work out? Not well as we shall see.

When Abram was eighty-seven, he and Hagar had a child, and he named him Ishmael. An angel of the Lord had told Sarai that his name was to be Ishmael and that he "*would be a wild donkey of a man, his hand will be against everyone, and everyone's hand would be against him, and he will live to the east of all his brothers*" (Genesis 16:12). That would make Ishmael an inhabitant of the desert and mountainous country east of the land of Canaan, east of the Jordan River. The Bible tells us that many troubles arose from Ishmael's people toward the future Israelites. That is an early example of what disobeying God or taking matters into one's own hands can lead to.

Thirteen years later, God gave Abram and Sarai a son. "*So Sarai conceived and bore a son to Abram in his old aged, at the appointed time of which God had spoken to him. And Abram called the name of his son Isaac*" (Genesis 21:2–3) At this point, God said to Abram, "Your name from henceforth will be Abraham." He also told Sarai her name would be Sarah.

After Isaac was weaned, Sarah took note of Ishmael and told Abraham to drive out Hagar and her son. Ishmael was Abraham's firstborn and had the first right of inheritance. Sarah wanted this right of inheritance for her son, Isaac. This distressed Abraham, but God told him to listen to Sarah and send them away. The

Bible says Ishmael lived in the wilderness and became an archer, and his mother took a wife for him from the land of Egypt, where she was from originally. The rest, as they say is history, as Ishmael's descendants, have plagued the Israelites ever since.

In Genesis 22, God decided to test Abraham to see if Abraham trusted Him. God told Abraham to take Isaac, his son, into the wilderness and offer him up as a burnt offering to God. The place God told Abraham to take Isaac was the Land of Moriah. Abraham and the lad, Isaac, went up to the high place in the land, Mount Moriah, and set about building an altar and gathering wood for a fire. Isaac asked his father where the lamb for the sacrifice was, and Abraham said not to worry, God would provide. Abraham then took Isaac and tied him to the altar as to sacrifice him and even lifted his knife to slay Isaac when God intervened. An angel spoke to Abraham and said, "*Abraham, do not stretch out your hand against the lad and do nothing to him, for now I know that you fear God, since you have not withheld your son, your only son, from me*" (Genesis 22:12).

What an incredible story! So early on in the Bible, God is prophesying the death of his only son, Jesus, as a sacrifice for our sins by having Abraham offer up his son as a sacrifice. Another amazing thing about this is that the city of Jerusalem was built centuries later on and around Mount Moriah, which is the very spot where Jesus, God's only son, was slain on the cross of Calvary as a sacrifice for our sins.

While we are on the subject of Abraham, let us visit the story of Sodom and Gomorrah, one of those strange stories we encounter in the Bible. I include this story to illustrate the results of sin, and as we shall see throughout the history of the Jews, there were lots of sin and many types of Christ whom God sent to redeem or rescue His people.

Sodom and Gommorah

Abraham and his nephew, Lot, became very prosperous in their new land, and when their livestock began vying for the same pastures, Abraham thought it best that they part ways and live away from each other. Abraham even gave Lot his choice of the lands. Of course, Lot took the best-looking, most productive pasture lands for himself, the valley of the Jordan River. So Lot departed from where he and Abraham were living. In Genesis 13:12, we find that Lot moved his tents as far as Sodom, which was believed to have been on the southwest corner of the Dead Sea.

The Bible records that the Lord visited Abraham on several occasions to tell Abraham what he was going to do. The most frequent message was that He would give Abraham a son, which He did. He also told Abraham that his descendants would find themselves in a strange land, where they would be enslaved and oppressed four hundred years.

One day, the Lord visited Abraham with three angels in the form of men. He told Abraham, one, that within a year, Sarah would give birth to a son. Sarah was nearby in their tent and overheard this conversation, and she laughed. Bear in mind that Sarah is eighty-nine years old at this time, so this statement sounded preposterous. She probably thought, *I've heard this before, and it hasn't happened yet, and at my age, really?* The angel heard her laugh and asked her why she laughed. Sarah denied laughing because she was afraid. The second thing the Lord told Abraham was that the people of Sodom were crying out to Him because of the rampant evil which was occurring there, and they were going there to see for themselves. If it were true, the Lord would destroy the place.

Abraham was alarmed at this announcement as his thoughts went to his nephew, Lot, who lived at Sodom. Not wanting his kinsman to suffer the wrath of God, Abraham began to bargain with God (the angels), asking if He would wipe out the whole population, even though there were some who were upright people. Abraham said, "Will you sweep away the righteous along with the wicked?" So Abraham negotiated with God not to destroy all the inhabitants if there were found as few as ten people who were righteous.

The men (angels) then departed for Sodom. Lot saw them coming and went out to meet them. Lot entreated the men to come and stay in his abode, but they said they would spend the night in the town square. It is likely that the angels wanted to see and judge the activities of the town-up close. Lot urged them strongly to stay in the safety of his house, and the men agreed. Later in the evening, the men of the city surrounded Lot's house and called to Lot to bring out these visiting men so that they might have sex with them. Lot went out and implored the men not to act wickedly and even offered his two daughters to them. But the townsmen rejected his offer and threatened to treat Lot worse than they were going to treat the visiting men.

The angels had seen and heard enough. They pulled Lot into the house and struck the townsmen with blindness so they could not find the doorway. Then the angels told Lot to take his family away from Sodom for they were going to destroy it because God had heard their outcry. Lot took his wife and two daughters, and they departed from Sodom. The angels cautioned them not look behind them and not to stay anywhere in the valley but escape to the mountains, lest they be destroyed along with Sodom. When they were well away from the area, the Lord rained fire and brimstone on the cities of Sodom and Gomorrah and destroyed them. Lot's wife turned around to watch the show, and she was turned into a pillar of salt (from Genesis 19).

I think there are two reasons this story is the Bible. First, God is a holy God. As the prophet Habakkuk says later in the Old Testament, *"God cannot look upon sin, His eyes are too pure to look on evil. He cannot tolerate wrongdoing"* (Habakkuk 1:12). In this case, the wrong-doing was sexual sin. Whether it was willful homosexuality or forced sex with other men, we do not know. God did say later in Leviticus 18:22, *"You shall not lie with a male as one lies with a female; it is an abomination."* The Levitical laws were written to expound on the Ten Commandments, which were given to the Israelites about five hundred years after this event in Sodom. Sinful activity was rampant in Sodom, so God punished the people for their abominations. God is illustrating here that sin comes with a price. The name Sodom is synonymous with wickedness and is referred to eleven times in the Bible in addition to its origin in Genesis and alludes to the price of sin.

When we sin, we can expect consequences. The consequences may occur outwardly or in ways known only to ourselves. However, God is ready to forgive us if we simply *"confess with our mouths the Lord Jesus and believe in our heart that God has raised Him from the dead"* (Romans 10:9). Then we have salvation and a renewed relationship with God.

The second reason I think this story is in the Bible is genealogy. After Lot and his daughters were saved from the destruction of Sodom, because there were no men available for the daughters, they made their father drunk and had sex with him. The firstborn had a son whom she named Moab. Moab became the father of the Moabites. Centuries later, Ruth, a Moabitess woman, married Boaz from Judah. They produced a son named Obed, the grandfather of David, whose ancestral line produced the incarnate Jesus.

Isaac and Jacob

The book of Genesis is the well-known book of the creation of the earth, man, animals, etc. People generally do not know all the stories of the interesting, sometimes evil and oftentimes great, men who were types of Christ written of in Genesis. We will spend a good deal of time in Genesis because there are many such characters therein. Abraham acted as a type of Christ by intervening with God to save his nephew, Lot, and his family from destruction. Jesus, by his death on the cross, saves us from the punishment that is required as a result of our sin.

The Bible was written to show God's great love for all people, regardless if they were evil and seemingly unlovable. The stories and events in the Bible are there to give examples of God's redemptive plan to bring people back to Him. Ultimately, God sent the Messiah, Jesus Christ, His Son, to earth to redeem us from our sin. So let us take a look at some of the types of Christ.

Isaac was not the only son of Abraham. Abraham took other wives and had sons by them. But Isaac was the one through whom God would bless Abraham with by making him a great nation and the one through whom Jesus would eventually be born. When Isaac was about forty years old, Abraham sent a servant back to Padden-Aram, in Upper Mesopotamia, from where Abraham had originally come, to find a wife from his kinsmen for Isaac. Abraham did not want Isaac to marry a local woman. The servant brought back Rebekah, the daughter of Bethuel and sister to Laban, and Isaac married her. Rebekah was barren some twenty years, so Isaac prayed to the Lord on her behalf. The Lord answered him, and Rebekah conceived twins.

Rebekah gave birth to twin boys, Esau and Jacob, in order of their birth. As the boys grew into young men, Rebekah favored Jacob, while Esau was the firstborn of the twins and was favored by Isaac. Being the first-born, Esau was in line for Isaac's blessing, which meant the lion's share of the inheritance. Rebekah wanted that blessing for Jacob, and so when Isaac was old and near death, she set about arranging a fraud to ensure that Jacob would receive the blessing from Isaac.

In his old age, Isaac had become near blind, proba-bly from cataracts. One day, he told Esau to go and kill some wild game and make for him a savory stew, and then he would bestow his blessing on him. Rebekah overheard this conversation, and when Esau departed to go hunting, Rebekah quickly conceived a plan to deceive Isaac and get the blessing for her favorite son, Jacob. Esau was an extremely hairy man, so Rebekah told Isaac to quicky kill one of the sheep in their flock. She took meat from the sheep Isaac had killed and prepared a savory stew from it for Isaac. She then took wool from the sheep and attached it to Jacob's arms and body and sent him to Isaac's tent to complete the deception and obtain Isaac's one-time-only blessing for his heir. Jacob took the stew to Isaac, and the ruse worked, and Isaac put his blessing on Jacob.

Later, Esau returned from his hunt and went to his father to obtain the blessing of the firstborn. It soon became obvious that Isaac had been tricked into giving the blessing to Jacob.

Jacob, one of the early ancestors in Jesus's lineage, perpetrated an evil fraud to gain the coveted blessing from his father. The name Jacob became synonymous with the term deceiver. Esau bore a grudge against Jacob because of the blessing his father had bestowed upon him, and Esau said to himself, "The days of mourning for my father are near, then I will kill my brother, Jacob." His words were overheard by a servant, who reported them to Rebekah. So Rebekah told Jacob to flee to Haran to her brother Laban until Esau's anger subsided. Recall that Haran was about five hundred miles away and was the land that Abraham had come from, also the land to which Isaac had obtained his wife, Rebekah. Rebekah told Isaac that Jacob went to Haran to find a wife since they did not want him to marry any of the local women in the area. Isaac thought that was a great idea.

So Jacob went to the land of his ancestors in Padan-Aram. When he arrived at Haran, one of the first people he saw was Rachel, the daughter of Laban, his uncle.

When Jacob saw Rachel, his heart raced with excitement, for he saw that she was very beautiful. Jacob told them that he was a relative of her father, the son of her aunt Rebekah. Rachel took off running to her father to tell him the news of Jacob's arrival. Laban was very happy to hear this news and went to meet his nephew. He embraced Jacob, kissed him, and brought him to his house (which was most likely a spacious tent). So Jacob stayed with Laban for a month.

Jacob was not a lazy fellow and pitched in to help with all the work that is required in the running of a successful livestock-raising enterprise. Laban was pleased and said to Jacob, "Shall you work for nothing? Tell me what shall your wages be." Now Laban had two daughters: Leah, the older one; and Rachel, the younger. Genesis says Leah's eyes were weak, which is a euphemism for not being so beautiful. Rachel was very beautiful of form and face. Now Jacob loved Rachel, so he said, "I will serve you seven years for your younger daughter, Rachel."

Laban said, "Sounds good to me. Better to you than to one of the locals."

After Jacob worked faithfully and hard for seven years, he said to Laban, "Give me my wife, for my time is completed, that I may go into her."

Laban then made a feast with lots of wine and spirits and celebrating. Jacob got drunk. In the evening, Laban took his daughter, Leah, to Jacob's tent, and Jacob excitedly went into her. The next morning, when Jacob was awake and sober, he saw that the woman he had been with during the night was not Rachel, but it was Leah, the weak-eyed older sister.

Man, was Jacob mad! He said to Laban, "What have you done to me? Was it not for Rachel that I served with you? Why have you deceived me?" Now there is an interesting turnabout: Laban was also a deceiver and had deceived the deceiver, Jacob. Deception must have run in their blood.

But Laban said, "It is not customary to marry off the younger before the firstborn. Complete the week of this one, and we will give you the other one also for your service of another seven years." So Jacob was pleased with this two-for-one deal, and after a week's service, Laban gave him Rachel for his wife. Laban also gave to each of his daughters a maid: to Leah, he gave

Zilpah; and to Rachel, he gave Bilhah. So Jacob went in to Rachel, and he served Laban for another seven years.

Now the Lord saw that Leah was unloved so He opened her womb. In other words, God made her very fertile, but He closed the womb of Rachel so that she could not have children. So Leah conceived and bore a son and named him Reuben. Leah said, "Because the Lord has heard that I am unloved, He has therefore given me this son." Leah conceived three more times and had three boys whom she named Simeon, Levi, and Judah. Then she stopped bearing children for a season.

Rachel was not very happy with her childless state, so Rachel offered her maid, Bilhah, to Jacob in order to have children she could call hers. Jacob and Bilhah produced two sons who were named Dan and Naphtali. Jacob and Zilpah then produced two sons named Gad and Asher. Leah then bore Jacob two more sons from her own womb and named them Issachar and Zebulon. Then Leah produced a daughter, whom she named Dinah. Remember this daughter as she will have a role in some interesting, if not evil, occurrence in the future.

Then God remembered Rachel, which is another way to say that God decided to bless Rachel with a son from her own womb because God never fails to carry out his promises. So Rachel conceived and bore a son, and she said, "God has taken away my reproach."

She named him Joseph, saying, "May the Lord give me another son" (from Genesis 30). Jacob produced eleven sons in Haran, who were part of God's promise to Abraham and to Jacob that he would make of them a great nation. A twelfth son would be born years later to Rachel in Canaan, and they would form the heads of the twelve tribes of Israel.

At this point, Jacob decided it was time to move away on his own and said to Laban, "Send me away that I may go to my own place and to my own country. Give me my wives and my children for whom I have served you, and let me depart for you, yourself, know the service which I have rendered you." After some bargaining in which it was agreed that Laban did not have all that much before Jacob came to Haran, Laban finally relented and said, "Name your wages, and I will give it."

So Jacob said, "If you will do this one thing for me, I will again pasture and keep your flock. Let me pass through your entire flock today, removing from there every speckled and spotted sheep, and every black one among the lambs, and the spotted and speckled among the goats, and such shall be my wages." In other words, Jacob said he wanted all the sheep and goats that were not solid white. Jacob said to Laban, "If you ever see a white sheep or goat among my flock, you may consider it stolen." Laban said, "Sounds good. Let it be as you say." Too bad Laban had not been paying attention.

Jacob, the deceiver, now using his knowledge of the sheep's mating tendencies, greatly multiplied his flocks, while Laban's flocks languished and were not nearly as numerous.

Soon, Jacob discerned that Laban's attitude was not favorable toward him, as formerly. The Lord then said to Jacob, "Return to the land of your fathers and to your relatives, and I will be with you." Then Jacob arose and put his children and his wives upon camels, and he drove away all his livestock and all his property he had acquired to go to the land of Canaan to his father, Isaac.

Jacob had some fears about returning to the land of his father, thinking Esau still wanted to kill him. But when he arrived in Canaan, he found that Esau bore no grudge, and Esau had been blessed richly with livestock and servants as had Jacob. Esau happily welcomed his brother home.

Jacob, now called Israel, went and camped outside the city of Shechem and bought a piece of land there. He erected an altar there and called it El-Elohe-Israel, which means "God, the God of Israel" (the God of Jacob, not the future country).

Remember Dinah, the daughter born to Leah? She becomes an important player at this time. She went out to visit the daughters of the land, and when Shechem, the son of Hamor the Hivite, the prince of the land, saw her, he took her and lay with her by force. He was deeply attracted to Dinah, the daughter of Israel, and he loved the girl and spoke tenderly to her. So Shechem spoke to his father Hamor and said, "Get me this young girl for a wife."

When Israel heard that Shechem had defiled his daughter, he was exceedingly angry. The sons of Israel also were incensed when they came in from the fields and learned of it.

Hamor came and spoke with them, saying, "The soul of my son Shechem longs for your daughter. Please give her to him in marriage and intermarry with us. Give your daughters to us and take our daughters for yourselves. So then, you shall live with us, and the land be open before you. Live and trade in it and acquire property in it." Shechem also said to Dinah's father and brothers, "If I find favor in your sight, then I will give whatever you say to you." But Israel's sons answered Shechem and his father, Hamor, with deceit, and said to them, "We cannot do this thing, to give our sister to one who is uncircumcised, for that would be a disgrace to us. Only on these conditions will we consent to you. If you will become like us, in that every male of you be circumcised, then we will give our daughters to you, and we will take your daughters for ourselves, and we will live with you and become one people. But if you do not agree to be circumcised, then we will take our daughter and go." This seemed reasonable to Hamor and Shechem, so they accepted the offer.

Hamor and Shechem returned to their people and explained all the benefits there would be if they joined the family of Dinah. It seemed reasonable and good to them as well. All the men in the city of Shechem submitted to circumcision. On the third day, when all the men were in great pain from their circumcision, two of Israel's sons, Simeon and Levi, came upon the city unawares with the edge of the sword and killed every male, including Hamor and his son, Shechem. They took Dinah from Shechem's house and returned home. Israel's sons then came upon the city and looted it because they had defiled their sister. They took flocks, herds, donkeys, and all that was in the city and in the field, and they captured and looted all their wealth and all their little ones and their wives.

Then Israel said to Simeon and Levi, "You have made me odious among the inhabitants of the land, among the Canaanites and the Perizzites, and my men being few in number, they will gather together against me and attack me, and I shall be destroyed, I and my household."

Simeon and Levi replied, "They should not have treated our sister as a harlot."

The tribe of Levi, many centuries later, would be appointed by God to be the priestly tribe of Israel.

I have included this story of Dinah because of a recurring theme. Deceitfulness is a sin that we have seen in Abraham, Isaac, Jacob, and now Jacob's sons.

Although not one of the so-called seven deadly sins, deceit can have deadly consequences, as we have seen. I see similarities in the story of Dinah and the woman caught in adultery and brought to Jesus in the New Testament Gospel of John. Both events occurred in a patriarchal society. Neither woman had a voice. We do not know the details of either story. There was sexual sin in both cases, and according to unwritten law, in Dinah's case and Mosaic law in the adultery case, there were dire consequences called for.

We see nothing in this story of deceitful, greedy people in Israel's family that resembles Jesus or His actions. Jesus taught forgiveness, not revenge. In the New Testament, Jesus said to the woman caught in adultery, which according to Levitical law, required stoning of both parties, "I do not condemn you. Go and sin no more."

Israel was in the direct ancestry of Jesus. Yet he would not be a sterling example of being righteous, at least in his early years.

Some time later, God told Israel to go up to Bethel and live there and make an altar there to God. Israel said to his household and to all who were with him, "Put away the foreign gods which are among you and purify yourselves and change your garments and let us arise and go up to Bethel." Later on, when they departed from Bethel to go to Hebron to see his aged father, Rachel, who was advanced with child, went into labor and gave birth to Benjamin, the twelfth son born to Israel. The birth was too much for Rachel, and she died and was buried near what is today Bethlehem. Benjamin was the head of the twelfth tribe of Israel.

Joseph

Now we move on to a discussion of one of the sons of Jacob and a type of Christ, Joseph. Even though Joseph was not in the lineage of Jesus, he was an incredibly important person in the history of the Israelites and, as a type of Christ, was instrumental in the preservation of the Jewish people in Egypt.

Rachel was Jacob's, now Israel's, favorite wife, his first love. When Rachel finally brought forth her first son, Joseph, he became Israel's favorite son. In Genesis 37, the story of Joseph begins. Joseph was about seventeen years old and was pasturing the flock with his brothers. As Joseph was the youngest and the favorite, Israel had a special varicolored coat made for him. His brothers saw that their father loved Joseph more than them. Therefore, they hated him and did not have a close relationship with him.

Once Joseph had a dream, and he told it to his brothers, infuriating them. He said, *"I dreamed we were binding sheaves in the field, and my sheaf rose up and stood erect, and your sheaves gathered around and bowed down to my sheaf.' His brothers asked to him, 'Are you actually going to rule over?"* (Genesis 37:7–8) So they hated him even more for his dreams and for his words.

Then Joseph had another dream and related it to his brothers. *"'I dreamed that the sun and the moon and eleven stars were bowing down to me.' He told it to his father who rebuked him and said, 'What is this dream that you have had? Shall I and your mother and your brothers actually come to bow ourselves down before you to the ground?"* (Genesis 37:9–10).

Later on, when Joseph's brothers were pasturing the flock a great distance from the home, Israel sent Joseph to check on their welfare. His brothers saw him coming afar off and began to plot against him to put him to death. Reuben said, "Let us not take his life, nor shed any blood. Throw him into this pit that is in the wilderness, but do not lay hands on him." Reuben had plans to rescue him out of their hands to restore him to his father. Remember, Reuben was the oldest brother and perhaps the wisest.

Joseph came sporting his coat of many colors, and his brothers stripped him of it and threw him into an empty pit. While they sat down to eat a meal, the brothers saw a caravan of Midianites coming from Gilead, their camels laden with spices, and headed down to Egypt. Reuben was away watching the sheep and was unaware of what transpired next.

Judah came up with the idea to be rid of Joseph without harming him—namely to sell Joseph to the Midianites. They pulled him out of the pit and sold him to the Midianites for twenty shekels of silver. Thus, the Midianites took Joseph down to Egypt. When Reuben found out what his brothers had done, he was furious, but there was nothing he could do.

The brothers slaughtered a goat and dipped Joseph's coat in the blood and brought it to their father and said, "We found this. Please examine it to see whether it is your son's coat or not."

Israel examined it and said, "It is my son's coat. A wild beast has devoured him." Israel tore his clothes and put sackcloth on his loins and mourned for his son many days.

Meanwhile, the Midianites sold Joseph in Egypt to Potiphar, pharaoh's officer, the captain of the body-guard. The Lord was with Joseph, so he became a successful man in the house of his master, the Egyptian. Potiphar saw that the Lord was with Joseph and that the Lord caused all that he did to prosper in his hand. Joseph became his personal servant, and Potiphar made him overseer of his house. All that he owned he put in Joseph's charge.

Through an incredible set of circumstances, including the imprisonment of Joseph, which only God could have accomplished, Joseph became administrator over all of Egypt, second in charge behind the pharaoh. You must read the account in Genesis, chapters 37 to 50 to appreciate it and understand its significance. Pharaoh gave him Asenath, the daughter of Potiphera, priest of On, as his wife. Joseph was just thirty years old and the chief administrator of all Egypt's affairs.

God had made Joseph a key part of his plan to save Israel and his family from dying from a famine that was to occur in that part of the world. Egypt would have bumper crops of grain for seven years, and Joseph was put in charge of storing grain to get Egypt through the seven years of famine which were to follow. During this time, two sons were born to Joseph by Asenath, the daughter of the priest of On. He named the firstborn Manasseh, for he said, "God has made me forget all my trouble and all my father's household." He named the second Ephraim, for he said, "God has made me fruitful in the land of my affliction." These sons, Manasseh and Ephraim, are important because many years later, they would be considered as two of the twelve tribes of Israel, taking the place of Joseph, who had for all intents and purposes become an Egyptian, and Levi, whose inheritance was the priesthood and not territory.

Then there came seven years of famine, not just in Egypt, but in all nearby lands. Joseph opened all the storehouses and sold to the people of all the earth who came to Egypt to buy grain. In Canaan, Israel saw that there was grain in Egypt, and he told his sons to go there and buy some for us "so that we may live and not die." Then ten brothers of Joseph went down to buy grain from Egypt. Israel did not send Joseph's brother Benjamin because he was afraid that harm might befall him.

When Joseph's brothers came and bowed down to him, he recognized them, but they did not recognize their brother. He demanded to know where they had come from. They told him they came from the land of Canaan to buy food. Joseph accused them of being spies, come to look at the undefended parts of our land.

Joseph continued to question them to find out if his father was still alive. They said their father was still alive, and they also had a younger brother who was also back in Canaan. Joseph was overcome by his emotions and said to his brothers, "I am your brother Joseph, whom you sold into Egypt. Do not be angry with yourselves because you sold me here. It was God's plan to preserve life."

"*Hurry and bring your father and all your families here. You shall live in the land of Goshen. There I will provide for you, for there are still five years of famine to come*" (Genesis 45:9–18, paraphrased). This is my favorite passage in all the Bible. It is a foreshadowing of Jesus's coming, the Son of God, who would come to preserve lives of all who would believe in him for the redemption of their sins. Joseph was a Type of Christ, who God used in a mighty and miraculous way to preserve his people, the people of Israel.

There is nothing more precious or emotional than the reuniting of family members who have been apart from each other for a long time. Family reunions are a time of rejoicing and even tears. God and the angel's rejoice when anyone makes the decision to believe in Jesus Christ to be the forgiver of their sins, to be their Savior, and be united in the family of God.

So Israel and his family, a total of seventy people in all, moved to Egypt and were settled in the Land of Goshen, where their descendants remained for four hundred years. After Joseph died, other pharaohs ruled in Egypt and had no appreciation for the work that Joseph had done in years past. In fact, they enslaved the Israelites and were cruel taskmasters over them. It was for this reason that the Israelites cried out to God to deliver them from the hands of the Egyptians.

Judah

Within the early part of the story of Joseph is a short story regarding Judah, the thirdborn of Israel's twelve sons. We saw earlier that he was complicit in getting rid of his brother, Joseph. One story in particular from Genesis 38 is interesting, seeing that Judah was in the direct lineage of Jesus.

Judah took a wife of a daughter of a Canaanite. She conceived and bore three sons: Er, Onan, and Shelah. Judah took a wife for his son, Er. Her name was Tamar.

Er was evil in the sight of God, and God took his life. Jewish tradition calls for the surviving brother to go in to the widow and raise up children for his brother's heritage. So Onan went in to lie with Tamar, but he wasted his seed on the ground because he did not want to give offspring to his brother. This displeased God, so God took his life.

Judah no doubt was hesitant to give Tamar to his third son after seeing what had happened to his first two sons. He told Tamar to live in his house until his other son was old enough. He had no intention of letting Shelah, his third and only remaining son, go in to her.

After a time, Judah's wife died. When the time of mourning was over, Judah traveled to Timnah to shear his sheep. Tamar disguised herself as a prostitute and placed herself in Judah's path to Timnah. When Judah passed by Tamar, he did not recognize her and turned aside to her and negotiated to lie with her in exchange for one of his sheep. Since Judah did not have a sheep with him, Tamar asked for a pledge, so Judah gave her his staff and signet ring.

When Judah came to his sheep, he sent his servant back with a sheep to redeem his staff and signet ring. The servant went, but the woman (Tamar) could not be found. Judah said to let her keep the staff and ring, lest he become a laughing stock. Tamar conceived from this union and became pregnant with twins.

About three months later, Tamar began to show; it was reported to Judah that his daughter-in-law was pregnant by harlotry. Judah said to bring her out for her to be burned. But Tamar brought out Judah's staff and ring and said, "Not so fast, fellows. I am pregnant by the man whose staff and ring these are."

Judah had to admit. "She is more righteous than I, in as much as I didn't give her to my son, Shelah" (Genesis 38:26).

Tamar gave birth to twins and named them Perez and Zereh. It was through Perez that the ancestral line of the Lord Jesus Christ proceeded. And we see in Judah for the second time, if not sinful, very questionable behavior.

Judah was one of the twelve tribes of Israel and was the name of the territory that his tribe inhabited when they entered the Promised Land from Egypt. When the Bible speaks of the lion of Judah in Revelation, it speaks of Jesus the conquering and victorious king. Jesus is the lion of the tribe of Judah.

CHAPTER 2

EXODUS

The book of *Exodus* tells the story of the freeing of the Israelites from their long enslavement by the Egyptians and their long journey back to their original home, the Promised Land, the land God promised Abraham centuries before. God chose Moses to affect their release from the Egyptians. Moses was a key figure in the history of the Jews, a descendant of Levi, who later would be known as the head of the priestly tribe. It was to Moses that God gave the Ten Commandments, the standard by which the Jews were to live and have a right relationship with God.

After nearly four hundred years in captivity, the Israelites, even though they were brutally abused as slaves, were so rapidly reproducing that the pharaoh ordered all Hebrew males be killed at their birth. When Moses was born, he was placed in a basket in the Nile River by his mother to hide him, that he might survive the pharaoh's edict. Pharaoh's daughter found him while bathing in the river. Moses's sister, Miriam, was watching nearby and offered to find the baby a wet nurse. She brought her mother as the wet nurse, so Moses's birth mother nursed him while he was raised in pharaoh's royal court. Moses received the best education available.

When Moses was about forty years old, he saw an Egyptian violently abusing a Hebrew youth. Seeing no one around, Moses killed the Egyptian and buried him in the sand. The incident became known to pharaoh, and pharaoh ordered that Moses be killed. Moses fled Egypt to Midian, in Sinai, the northern extent of Egypt. Moses found a wife there and lived there for forty years, tending sheep for his father-in-law, Jethro. One day, Moses observed a bush that was burning, but it was not being consumed. Moses approached the bush, and a voice came from the bush and spoke Moses's name, saying that it was God who was talking with him. God told Moses that he was to return to Egypt to be His instrument to free the enslaved Hebrews and lead them to the Promised Land.

Moses reluctantly obeyed God and returned to Egypt to talk pharaoh into letting the Hebrews go. Forty years had passed, so the current pharaoh did not know of Moses's earlier history in Egypt. Moses asked pharaoh to let the Hebrews go about three days journey away to pray and make sacrifices to their God, Yahweh. Pharaoh would not listen. God used Moses to bring ten different plagues or disasters upon the Egyptian people to force pharaoh to let the Hebrews go to worship their God. Pharaoh told Moses each time that if he would remove the plague, he would let the Hebrew people go and worship. But each time the plague was removed, pharaoh changed his mind and would not let the Hebrews go. After the ninth plague, pharaoh told Moses that if he came back to see him again, Moses would be executed.

God told Moses that he would bring about one more plague on Egypt and that they were to pack up and be ready to move out. That plague was what we know as the Passover, where all the firstborn in Egypt would be killed by the death angel. That plague convinced Pharaoh to let the Hebrews go to their place of worship. When the new day revealed all the deaths of Egypt's sons, pharaoh said the Hebrews could go. This last calamity was called the Passover because all Hebrew families were spared by the death angel if they put the blood of a lamb on their doorposts. When the angel saw the blood of a lamb on the doorposts, he would "pass over" that dwelling and spare it the loss of the firstborn.

This Passover is so important in the history of the Jews that it is celebrated every year throughout the world by Jews.

Soon after pharaoh released the Hebrews to go on their journey, he regretted it and sent his soldiers after them to bring them back. The soldiers caught up with the Hebrews at the shore of the Red Sea, and the Hebrews thought their short sabbatical was over, having no place to escape. God had other plans, of course, and used Moses as his instrument to perform the miracle of parting the Red Sea so the Hebrews could escape and continue their journey back to the Promised Land. The Egyptian army made the mistake of following the Hebrews between the walls of water, and when the Hebrews exited the passage into the Sinai, God released the waters, and the entire army of pharaoh perished.

Moses, who had committed murder over forty years earlier, returned to Egypt as a type of Christ whom God used to free his people from their bondage to the Egyptians. As Jesus was sent to earth to be the Savior of the world, Moses was a savior to the Jews in Egyptian bondage by rescuing, teaching, and preserving them until they were in the Promised Land. Jesus Christ is our Savior and preserver until we reach our promised land, heaven. The children of Israel, estimated to number up to a million, were now free from their enslavement to the Egyptians and had a long and arduous journey ahead. They were without a code of conduct of their own, so God saw fit to provide them a set of rules for their personal conduct as he did by giving Moses the law tablets on Mount Sanai.

Moses was to take these commandments and teach them to the people. Foremost of all the commandments are the Ten Commandments. The first four of the Ten Commandments pertained to the relationship that the people were to have with God Himself:

1. *You shall have no other Gods before me.*
2. *You shall not make for yourself an idol, or any likeness of what is in heaven above or on the earth beneath or in the water under the earth.*
3. *You shall not take the name of the Lord your God in vain.*
4. *Remember the Sabbath Day, to keep it holy.*

The other six commandments governed the relationship of the people to each other.

5. *Honor your father and your mother.*
6. *You shall not commit murder.*
7. *You shall not commit adultery.*
8. *You shall not steal.*
9. *You shall not bear false witness against your neighbor.*
10. *You shall not covet your neighbor's wife or his property.* (Exodus 20:2–17)

In Matthew chapter 22, Jesus was asked, "Master, which is the great commandment in the law?" Jesus replied, "Thou shalt love the Lord thy God with all thy heart, and with all thy soul, and with all thy mind.

This is the first and great commandment, and the second is like unto it, thou shalt love thy neighbor as thyself. On these two commandments hang all the law and the prophets." In other words, strict obedience of these two laws covers everything. But we know that is not possible.

Fact: People sin. They do not honor God; they do not love others as they love themselves. That, in and of itself, does not relegate a person to hell or eternal darkness because God made a provision in that when we do sin, we can confess that sin to Him and restore our relationship with Him. Psalms 103:12 says, *"He will remove our sin from us as far as the east is from the west."* 1 John 1:9–10 states, *"If we confess our sins, He is faithful and just and will forgive us our sins and purify us from all unrighteousness. If we claim we have not sinned, we make Him out to be a liar and His word has no place in our lives."*

The Israelites had a logistical problem. They soon had eaten all the livestock they brought out of Egypt. God sent manna as dew from heaven to provide food for them. They grew tired of this manna—a type of bread—every day, so God sent quails to provide meat for them.

Exodus then tells how God instructed the Israelites, through Moses, to construct a tabernacle for Him so that God could dwell among them and be a constant reminder to the people that He was their God, and they were to have no other Gods before them. The Israelites needed something they could see to remind them of the presence and preeminence of God. God would not allow any man to see Him, for to see Him was to die. He gave Moses detailed instructions for a tabernacle to be built so that God could dwell among them without being seen. Only the high priest could enter that part of the tabernacle called the Holy of Holies, where God dwelt. Moses's brother, Aaron, was appointed by God as the first high priest. They were to build a special box to be called the Ark of the Covenant in which were placed the stone tablets of the commandments and a jar of manna. God dwelt above the ark in the Holy of Holies. There were specific rules for carrying the ark, and if anyone touched the ark with his hands, he was struck dead.

This, in itself, was a prophetic picture of Jesus Christ whom God, in essence, tabernacled to live among men for thirty-three years, the incarnate Christ. Today, our body is a tabernacle for the indwelling of the Holy Spirit, whom Jesus promised when he told his disciples that He would send a comforter or helper to always be with us when we have accepted Him as our Savior. In 1 Corinthians 6:19–20, the apostle Paul exhorted, *"Do you not know that your body is a temple of the Holy Spirit, who is in you, whom you have received from God? You are not your own; you were bought at a price. Therefore, honor God with your body."*

While there are no direct Messianic references to Christ in Exodus, Moses was Christlike in that he was a prophet, a priest, and a king. Although not a king, per se, Moses functioned as a ruler or leader of the Israelites until they reached the Promised Land. The exodus from Egypt is a symbol of our freedom from an old life of sin and identification of a new life in Christ. Moses's ministry as a high priest foreshadows the ministry of Christ as our high priest.

There were many times throughout the Old Testament when the Israelites were going through hard times. They questioned God, asking, *"Why have you deserted us? Why have you divorced us?"* God responded, *"I have not divorced you; you have divorced me. Return to me, confess your sins, and I will restore you"* (Jeremiah 3:11–14, paraphrased). The Psalmist David said, *"If I go ascend into the heavens or descend into the depth of the sea, you are there"* (Psalm 139). God is always there with us, but are we with Him?

CHAPTER 3

LEVITICUS, NUMBERS, AND DEUTERONOMY

The name *Leviticus* comes from the tribal name of Levi. Leviticus focuses on providing guidance to a newly redeemed people. Through Moses, God teaches the Israelites how to worship and fulfill their priestly calling.

In Exodus 15:26, God said, *"If you will give earnest heed to the voice of the Lord your God, and do right in his sight, and give ear to His commandments, and keep all His statutes, I will put none of these diseases on you which I have put on the Egyptians; for I, the Lord, am your healer."* In Leviticus, Moses expounds on the laws God gave him on Mount Sinai and actually gives them rules for morality, as well as for eating and cleanliness, all of which were to ensure their health and well-being.

While there are no character stories or prophetic verses in Leviticus, there are explanations of offerings

and feasts and rules for daily bodily care and mainte-
nance. The Hebrews were a mobile people and as such
required extra care, particularly because there were so
many people in close quarters. The offerings, feasts, and
sacrifices point to Jesus and allude to His character. For
example, the peace offering is a sacrifice of an animal
whose blood is sprinkled on the altar to atone for one's
sins. With this sacrifice comes peace with God. When
we accept the sacrifice of Jesus's blood on the cross as
payment for our sins, we have peace with God.

After expounding on the statutes concerning the
offerings and sacrifices, Moses gave laws on holiness
and health, often in minute detail. An interesting rule
given was that if a lizard fell into a cooking pot, the
pot was to be destroyed if earthenware and scoured if a
bronze pot. Lizards were considered unclean and could
cause sickness. Leviticus also has teachings on sexual
purity and when not to drink alcoholic beverages, such
as when they went to worship at the tent of meeting.

So we see Leviticus as more or less a guidebook for
daily living, both for health and being holy or Christlike
in our actions and relations to each other. Leviticus
11:44 says, *"For I am the Lord your God. Consecrate
yourselves therefore, and be holy; for I am holy."*

The book of *Numbers* covers the period of the
Israelites wandering in the wilderness, which lasted
forty years. Why did it take forty years to complete
what was ordinarily an eleven-day journey? The reason

was unbelief. Because they were going to an unknown land, God told Moses to send spies into the Promised Land and bring back a report of what was there. Moses chose twelve men, one from each tribe, to search out the land. When the twelve spies returned, they gave a report of great resources, fertility, and fruit. Regarding the people that lived in the promised land, there were giants and well-fortified cities. Ten of the spies said that they should not go there, that the obstacles were too great. However, two spies, Joshua and Caleb, said that they should certainly go up and possess the land because God was with them.

Because of their unbelief and grumblings at the spies' report, God decreed that the Israelites would wander in the wilderness for forty years during which time everyone twenty years of age and older who had grumbled against God would die. God struck down the ten disbelieving spies immediately and brought plagues on the Israelites for their stubborn disobedience and resistance to the leadership of Moses.

There are a number of allusions to Christ in the book of Numbers. The most obvious occurs in Numbers 21 when the people spoke against God, and God sent fiery serpents among them, causing many deaths. God told Moses to replicate a serpent out of bronze and mount it on a pole. When people looked up at the bronze serpent, they were healed and made impervious to the snakelike serpents. This is the representation of Christ to the people in the wilderness as Christ the Messiah was lifted up on the cross at Calvary. Jesus said, *"If I be lifted up from the earth, I will draw all men unto me"* (John 12:22).

In Numbers 24, we read the oracle of Balaam, who was a prophet of God who lived far to the east near the Euphrates River. Balak, King of Moab, was in fear of the Israelites who were defeating all Israelites they encountered as they moved north and were about to enter his land. Balak sent word to Balaam to curse the Israelites, but instead, Balaam blessed them. Within Balaam's oracle, he said, *"I see him, but not now. I behold him, but not near; A star shall come forth from Jacob, and a scepter shall arise from Israel, and shall crush through the forehead of Moab, and tear down all the sons of Sheth"* (verse 17). This oracle indicates that Moab will be defeated, but it is also believed by scholars to be a prophecy of the coming of the Messiah, who descended from the line of Jacob. The star refers to the star seen from the east by the Magi, who came and visited Jesus shortly after His birth in Bethlehem.

You might ask, "Why didn't God move the Israelites directly to the Promised Land instead of having them wander about for forty years?" The aforementioned reason of unbelief and disobedience is only part of the answer. Through time and experience, the Israelites had much to learn and become versed in before they entered Canaan and became separated by tribes over hundreds of square miles. Before they entered Canaan, they needed to develop a relationship with God and be obedient to Him. As we shall see in the book of Judges, even though leadership had passed from Moses to Joshua, their geographical spread created problems in receiving the guidance they needed from a central leader.

The book of *Deuteronomy* is essentially Moses's last messages to the children of Israel before they entered the promised land and before Moses died. The Israelites have now wandered in the wilderness for forty years as God decreed as a result of their lack of trust in Him. In these messages, Moses continued to teach them God's laws given to him on Mount Sinai. When we look for Jesus in Deuteronomy, we see Moses as a type of Christ in that he filled the role of king, priest, and prophet. Although not appointed as king, he, in reality, functioned as the ruler of the Israelites. As priest, he was the advocate with God for the people; and as prophet, he made two notable prophecies. In Deuteronomy 17, Moses said that when the Israelites entered the land that the Lord God gave them, they would want a king to rule over them. About 350 years would go by before the Israelites told Samuel the High Priest that they wanted a king, and Saul was anointed to rule over them. Moses prophesied of Jesus when he said in Deuteronomy 18:15, "*The Lord thy God will raise up for you a Prophet like me from among you, from your countrymen, you shall listen to him.*" That Prophet was Jesus.

When Moses finished speaking to his brethren all the laws and prophecies, God told him to go up on Mount Nebo, later known as Mount Pisgah, which over-looked the Promised Land toward the Mediterranean Sea, to "*die and be gathered to your people, because you broke faith with Me at the waters of Meribah-Kadesh in the wilderness of Zin*" (Deuteronomy 32:45–52). Moses died there, and God buried him in the land of Moab. I leave the account of Moses's breaking faith with God at Meribah-Kadesh for you to read.

CHAPTER 4

JOSHUA AND JUDGES

The book of *Joshua* is the first of twelve historical books and tells how Israel took possession of the Promised Land. The name Joshua, originally *Hoshea*, means salvation. In Greek, the name is *Iesous* or Jesus. Jesus is our salvation.

As the forty years of wandering came to a close and the Israelites actually traveled north to the Promised Land, they had to pass through areas inhabited by people who were not friendly toward them. Moses and Joshua took their cues from God and went into battle only when God told them to. After the departure of Moses, when the people wanted to go up and defeat the Amalekites, Joshua told them to wait. The people said, "God is with us. We will defeat them." But Joshua said, "No, God will not be with us." The people decided to fight anyway, and they suffered a great defeat at the hands of the Amalekites. Eventually, God led them to victory over all the foes they had to fight to get to Canaan, and at last they were poised to go into Canaan, which actually consisted of lands both east and west of the Jordan River.

The tribes of Gad and Reuben and the half tribe of Manasseh wanted to settle in areas east of the Jordan. Joshua allowed it with their promise that they would send their armies across the Jordan with the other tribes to help them defeat the inhabitants they would encounter. The half tribe of Manasseh and the other nine tribes were to cross over the Jordan River and occupy lands to the west.

Just across the Jordan River was the walled city of Jericho. In preparation for the coming invasion by the Israelites into Canaan, Joshua sent two spies to see what they would be up against when they went to capture their first stronghold, namely Jericho. These two spies went to Jericho and entered the house of a harlot named Rahab and lodged there. The first-century Roman-Jewish historian, Josephus, wrote that Rahab was an innkeeper, so it makes sense the spies might lodge in an inn. Owning an inn made it convenient for Rahab to be a harlot, which she may have been to supplement the meager income she received as innkeeper.

Some of the inhabitants of Jericho saw the two Israelite men come into Jericho and take up lodging at Rahab's inn and reported it to the authorities. The king of Jericho sent messengers to Rahab, telling her to bring out the two men, believing they had come to search out all the land. Rahab had hidden the two men. She told the king's messengers that the men had left, and she did not know where they had gone. She had brought them to the roof and hid them in some stalks of flax, which she had laid out there.

Rahab was familiar with the great military successes of the Israelites and wanted to be on their side. Rahab bargained with the spies to deal kindly with her family when they conquered Jericho. So the men agreed that when the Lord gave them the land, they would deal kindly with Rahab and her family. When it was safe, she let them down by a rope through the window and they escaped, for the house was on the city wall (Joshua 2).

God's plan for the capture of Jericho was for the Israelites to march around the city once a day for seven days with the Ark of the Covenant, and on the seventh day, they were to give a great shout and blow their trumpets. Joshua carried out the directions from God, and Jericho's walls came tumbling down. Rahab, the harlot, and her family were saved.

Isn't it amazing how God can use anyone, sinners or upright, to accomplish his desires? Some historians credit Rahab with being one of Israel's early saviors due to her allegiance to God and Israel and as the first non-Israelite person to ally with Israel. Rahab's knowledge of the Hebrew people's battle successes east of the Jordan River because of their God's power led her to protect the men sent by Joshua. She did not want to become a battle casualty, so she bargained with the spies and saved herself and her family. She and her family then integrated into the Jewish family. Rahab later married Salmon, who was the father of Boaz, the great grandfather of David in the genealogy of Jesus.

God used two women who were not Jewish to further his purposes and continue the line through which Jesus would be born. The first was Rahab and the second was Ruth, a Moabite woman, whom Boaz married and will be discussed later in the book of Ruth.

Joshua was also a type of Christ in that he succeeded Moses, the conveyor of the Mosaic law, and Christ succeeded the Mosaic law. Prior to Jesus, salvation was achieved through the works of (obedience to) the law. In Ephesians 2:8–10, Paul says, *"For by grace you have been saved through faith, and that not of yourselves, it is a gift of God; not as a result of works, that no one can boast. For we are His workmanship, created in Christ for good works, which God prepared beforehand, that we should walk in them."* We cannot get salvation by our works; salvation comes by faith. Without faith, no one can please God. *"Whoever comes to God must believe that he is real and that He rewards those who sincerely try to find him" (Hebrews 11:6).*

After the fall of Jericho, Joshua wasted little time in advancing to conquer the lands where the Israelites would settle. The lands the nine-and-one-half tribes would occupy west of the Jordan River extended from Kadesh-Barnea in the south to Mount Hermon, near present-day Lebanon, in the North, a distance of about two hundred miles. They were only able to conquer the peoples in the central mountainous areas. They were unable to defeat the inhabitants of the areas from the mountains to the coast, and these inhabitants were a thorn in the side of the Israelites for hundreds of years.

The book of *Judges* is important, not because of any ancestors of Jesus (there are none mentioned), but because God used various key people to do His bidding in rescuing the Israelites from the troubles they got into because of their disobedience. Each of the seventeen judges mentioned in this book symbolized and acted as a savior or type of Christ, either in rescuing the Hebrews from their captivities because of their disobedience to God or ruling over them to judge their complaints and disagreements. The final verse of the book of Judges serves as the theme of the book and the over 350-year period it covers.

> In those days, there was no king in Israel; everyone did what was right in his own eyes. (Judges 21:25)

After Jericho fell to Joshua, God instructed the Israelites to go in and take the land and told each tribe of Israel where they were to take their portion of the land of Canaan. He told them to drive out all the inhabitants before them and not to intermarry with them.

God gave to the tribe of Ephraim, which Joshua was from, land near the center of the land of Canaan, west of the Jordan River, and Joshua did as God instructed and drove out the inhabitants of the land. The boundaries of the twelve tribes were to extend to the Mediterranean Sea, but the Israelites were unable to drive out the inhabitants in the plains near the Mediterranean. These lands were inhabited primarily by Philistines and other Canaanite tribes. At various times during the next three-and-a-half centuries, the people surrounding the Israelites plagued them and even conquered some of their lands. God selected key individuals known as judges to deliver the Israelites from their tormentors and to regain sovereignty of their territories. Thus, God used the judges as types of Christ to be a savior of the Israelites from their enemies and to be spiritual deliverers.

After Joshua and his generation died, the people began to fall away from their relationship with God; they had no one like Moses or Joshua to guide them with direct leadership on a daily basis. The people of Israel intermarried with the inhabitants of Canaan, giving their daughters to the inhabitants and taking the inhabitants' daughters for their sons. This led to the Israelites abandoning Jehovah God and worshipping the foreign gods of their wives and husbands with whom they had intermarried. God's wrath burned against them, and so He allowed the foreigners to go into battle against and defeat the Israelites. The first of these conquerors were Mesopotamians.

Life was not good under their foreign captors. So the Israelites complained to God for help, and God would use a "judge" to raise an army under God's supervision to defeat the foreign captors. The first of these judges was Othniel, the son of Kenaz, Caleb's younger brother. Remember that Caleb was one of two spies of the Land of Canaan who, along with Joshua, brought back a good report and knew that God would win the victory for them over the Canaanites. Othniel raised an army from the tribe that God had chosen and went out and defeated the Mesopotamians (Judges 3:1–4).

The land had rest for forty years, and Othniel died. But Israel continued in their worship of foreign gods and doing evil in the sight of God. God allowed the Moabites under King Eglon to defeat Israel in battle. The Moabites, from the east and south across the Jordan River, took control of the people of Ephraim.

The Ephraimites served Eglon, king of the Moabites, for eighteen years. Then God appointed a judge, Ehud, to deliver the Israelites from the Moabites. Ehud secretly raised an army in preparation for the overthrow of the Moabites. Ehud went to visit Eglon, King of the Moabites, to give him a tribute. Ehud bound a two-edged knife inside of his right thigh. He delivered the tribute while Eglon was cooling in his roof chamber. After Ehud delivered the tribute, he told Eglon that he had a secret message for him. Eglon sent all his aides out of the chamber. Ehud approached to whisper to the king and took the knife from his right thigh with his left hand and plunged it into the belly of Eglon. Eglon was corpulent, so the knife's hilt was swallowed up by the fat of his belly. Ehud went out of the chamber and closed the chamber doors and escaped. He returned to his secretly formed army and took them and routed the Moabites from the land of the Israelites (Judges 3:12–30).

After eighty years of peace, the Lord gave the Israelites into the hands of Midian for seven years. The Midianites held complete power over Israel even so far as to destroy their crops and leave no sustenance and took all weapons from them. Israel cried out to the Lord for help. So God chose a man from the westerly half tribe of Manasseh named Gideon, the son of Joash, to deliver them.

When an angel visited and told him he was a valiant warrior and that the Lord was with them, Gideon said, "If that is true, why are we under the Midianites power? Where are all the miracles our fathers told us about favoring Israel?"

Then the angel, who was actually the Lord himself, said, "Go in your strength and deliver Israel from the Midianites."

Gideon surely thought this person was misinformed. So Gideon said, "How can I deliver Israel from the Midianites? I am too young and inexperienced."

But the Lord said to him, "Surely I will be with you, and you shall defeat Midian as one man."

Ever-skeptical Gideon said, "You have to prove to me that you are the Lord. I need a sign that you are the Almighty."

The Lord said, "All right, try me."

So Gideon prepared a meal for the angel. The angel said to put the food on a nearby rock, which Gideon did. The angel touched the food with his staff, and fire sprang up from the rock and consumed it. Miracle? Yes. Gideon was impressed, but not yet sure.

The Lord told Gideon to take his father's two bulls and build an altar to sacrifice them on. The wood for the altar was to come from the Asherah, a statue of the goddess the Midianites worshipped that he was to pull down. Gideon did it under the cover of darkness because he was afraid of his father and the men of the city.

The next morning, when the people saw that the Asherah was pulled down, they demanded, "Who did this thing?" After inquiring around, it was determined that Gideon, the son of Joash, had done it, and the men of the city wanted to kill him because he had torn down the Baal altar.

Joash defended Gideon by saying, "*Will you contend for Baal, or will you deliver him? Whoever will plead for Baal shall be put to death. If Baal is a god, let him contend for himself*" (Judges 6:31).

When the Midianites heard about this, they sent an army across the Jordan and camped in the valley of Jezreel. The spirit of the Lord came upon Gideon, and he sent messengers throughout his tribe and to three other tribes to get help; thousands of men rallied to his call. But Gideon said to the Lord, "I need a little more proof that you are the Lord and that you will deliver Israel through me. I will put a fleece of wool on the ground on the threshing floor, and tomorrow morning, if there is dew on the fleece only and it is dry all around it, then I will know it is you who has spoken."

The next morning, the fleece was loaded with water and the ground around it was dry. Gideon was still not fully satisfied, so he said, "Okay, tonight, let the fleece be dry and the ground all around it be wet." The next morning, the fleece was dry and the ground around it was very wet.

Then the Lord told Gideon that he had too many men to do battle; Israel will think they defeated the Midianites and will be boastful. Gideon told everyone who was trembling or afraid to go home. Twenty-two thousand people went home, leaving ten thousand. The Lord told Gideon there were still too many men. "Bring them down to the brook, and I will test them there. Those who lap the water as a dog laps, you can keep. Everyone else goes home." That left Gideon with only three hundred men. He separated the three hundred men into three companies of one hundred. He gave a trumpet and a pitcher with a lit torch inside to every man and said, "When we get very close to the Midianite camp, do as I do. When I blow the trumpet, you blow your trumpet. When I break my pitcher, you break your pitcher. Then cry out, 'For the Lord and for Gideon.'"

So they executed this plan, and they held their torches in their left hand and the trumpets in their right hand. They had no weapons to use against the Midianites, so the Lord set the Midianites against each other, killing each other with the sword. Gideon's men just held their torches high and blew their trumpets as the Lord sent the Midianites running in confusion (Judges 6:11–8:28).

Our God is an awesome God, and He is to be reverenced. But that does not mean we cannot converse with him and do some bargaining with Him. Remember when Abraham bargained with God not to destroy Sodom if there were righteous people there? With Gideon, we see that he questioned God quite pointedly, but fairly. And he told God that He had to prove that it was the Lord he was talking to.

In Isaiah 41, God spoke through the prophet Isaiah to the Israelites when they were being besieged by the Assyrians because of their idolatry, saying, *"Do not fear, for I am with you. I will strengthen you. Surely, I will help you. Surely, I will uphold you with my righteous right hand."* He said, *"Present your case, let us talk openly about this. You tell me what is going to happen, if you can"* (verse 21).

God will listen to us if we are serious and humble ourselves before Him. We can argue with God, but in the end, we have to be obedient to Him and do His will.

As a sidenote, around the year 1900, a group of Christian men gathered together to determine how they could do the work of the Lord and let God's power work in people's lives. They called themselves the Gideons. Their work was to distribute free-of-charge Bibles, the sword of the Lord. The Bibles are paid for by freewill offering by local churches all over the world. They are in approximately two hundred countries worldwide. One of their biggest outreaches is the placing of Bibles in hotel and motel rooms. It would be difficult to find a hotel or motel that does not have a Gideon's Bible in its rooms. Although it is the thousands of Gideons who are warriors for the Lord, it is the power of the Word and the Holy Spirit that changes people's hearts.

The last of the Judges I will discuss is probably the most well-known, and this story is a picture of the consequences of disobedience on a personal, individual level. This is the story of Samson from Judges 13–16.

After the forty-year peace following Gideon's (and God's) victory over Midian, the Israelites again did evil in the sight of God, and God gave them into the hands of the Philistines. So God produced another judge to punish their captors.

There was a certain man from the family of the tribe of Dan, whose name was Manoa, and his wife was barren and had borne no children. In the book of Judges, chapter 13, we read that an angel appeared to Manoa's wife and told her she would have a son. He instructed her that no razor was to come upon his head for he was to be a Nazarite to God from the womb and that he would deliver Israel from the Philistines.

Some people think that Samson's being called a Nazarite makes him kin to Jesus. However, Jesus was a Nazarene, being from Nazareth, not a Nazirite. The name Nazarite means especially consecrated to God.

The woman gave birth to a son and named him Samson, and the child grew up, and the Lord blessed him. God gave Samson extraordinary strength, allowing him to kill a lion with his bare hands, and later he killed one thousand Philistines using the jawbone of an ass as his only weapon. Samson married a Philistine woman. When his Philistine father-in-law gave his wife to someone else, Samson caught many foxes and tied burning torches to their tails and set them loose in Philistine's wheat fields and groves, and their crops were destroyed. When the Philistines found out Samson had done this, they burned the woman and her family. In response, Samson struck them ruthlessly with a great slaughter.

In time, it came about that Samson loved another Philistine woman whose name was Delilah. And the lords of the Philistines came up to her and said to her, "Entice him, and see where his great strength lies. See how we may overpower him that we may bind him to afflict him. Then we will each give you 1,100 pieces of silver." So Delilah pressed Samson daily to tell her where his great strength came from. Samson gave her several false versions until she finally wore him down, and he told her that his long hair, having never been cut, was the secret to his strength.

When Delilah saw that he had told her all that was in his heart, she sent for the lords of the Philistines, saying, "Come up once more, for he has told me all that is in his heart." Then the lords of the Philistines came up to her and brought the money in their hands. She made Samson to sleep on her lap, and she called for a man and had him shave off all his hair. She then called for the Philistines to come and take him.

The Lord had left him, and he was powerless to fight the Philistines. The Philistines seized him and gouged out his eyes, and they brought him down to Gaza and bound him with bronze chains, and he was a grinder in the prison. However, the hair of his head began to grow again.

Now the lords of the Philistines assembled to offer a great sacrifice to Dagon, their god, and to rejoice, for they said, "Our God has given Samson our enemy into our hands." When the people saw him, they praised their god, for they said, "Our god has given our enemy into our hands, even the destroyer of our country, who has slain many of us."

When they were in high spirits, they called for the blind Samson to be brought to amuse them. So Samson was brought from the prison, and he entertained them, and they made him stand between the pillars of the great assembly building. Then Samson said to the boy who was holding his hand, "Let me feel the pillars on which the house rests that I may lean against them."

Now the house was full of men and women, and all the lords of the Philistines were there. About three thousand men and women were on the roof, looking on while Samson was amusing them. Then Samson called to the Lord and said, "Oh Lord God, please remember me and please strengthen me just this time, O God, that I may at once be avenged of the Philistines for my two eyes."

And Samson grasped the two middle pillars on which the house rested and braced himself against them. Samson said, "Let me die with the Philistines!" And he bent with all his might against the pillars so that the house fell on the lords and all the people who were in it. The dead whom he killed at his death were more than those whom he killed in his life. Samson had judged Israel twenty years (from Judges 13–16).

The fact that during the period of the judges Israel had no king or ruler over them allowed for foreign nations or peoples to come in and take over their lands. The period of the judges ends with Samuel, who was also a priest to Israel. During his priesthood, the people finally demanded that they have a king, so God told Samuel to select a person to be their leader and anoint him king.

CHAPTER 5

RUTH

The story of Ruth occurs during the period of the judges. There is only a very weak allusion to Christ in the book when it speaks of Boaz being a kinsman redeemer, and thereby, a type of Christ. Boaz, as a kinsman of Naomi, the mother-in-law of Ruth, was able to redeem the property of Naomi, which included marrying Ruth, her daughter-in-law.

It is my belief that there is another purpose for including book of Ruth in the Bible and in this particular location in the Bible. That reason is genealogy. In Ruth chapter 4, Ruth bears a son to Boaz, and he is named Obed. Obed was the father of Jesse, who was the father of David, King of Israel and Judah, and author of 73 Psalms. Ruth 4:18–22 states the genealogy of Jesus from Perez, the son of Judah, to David, the son of Jesse. The next book in the Bible is 1 Samuel in which David comes on the scene. Samuel was also considered the last of the judges.

The story of Ruth is one of history's great love stories. Elimelech, along with his wife, Naomi, and their two sons, left Bethlehem of Judah and went to Moab because of a famine. The two sons married Moab women. After some time, Elimelech and the two sons died, leaving Naomi with the two daughters-in-law with no means of support. Naomi decided to return to Bethlehem, where she was the heir to Elimelech's property, apparently a small piece of land. She urged the daughters-in-law to stay in Moab and find new husbands. One daughter-in-law, Ruth, loved Naomi and could not be dissuaded from returning to Bethlehem with Naomi. Ruth said to Naomi, "*Where you go, I will go; where you lodge, I will lodge; your people shall be my people; your God will be my God; where you die, I will die*" (Ruth 1:16–17).

They arrived in Bethlehem in the beginning of the barley harvest. Naomi told Ruth to go to the field of Boaz, a kinsman, and glean some grain so that they would not starve. Boaz took note of Ruth and treated her lovingly, allowing her to generously glean and to be protected from harm. Naomi guided Ruth to attract Boaz to her and thereby provide future security for both of them. Boaz loved Ruth and wanted to marry her, but there was a kinsman who was closer to Naomi, who had the first right of refusal for Naomi's inheritance. Since Ruth was part of the right to inheritance, the other kinsman decided he did not want another woman, so he gave the rights to Naomi's inheritance to Boaz. Boaz then married Ruth, and they produced a son, whom they named Obed. Thus, Ruth became the second woman and non-Jew in the genealogy of Jesus.

CHAPTER 6

1 AND 2 SAMUEL

Late in the period of the judges, the people of Israel started complaining to God that they wanted a king to be over them so they could be like the kingdoms around them whose leaders exhibited an image of power, magnificence, and ceremony. Israel wanted a celebrity king to be a showpiece for their vanity and worldliness. But to God, this was a rejection of Him as their king and magnificent potentate. They wanted a person they could visually see and talk to.

The prophet Samuel was actually the last of the judges that were prominent in the role of leadership over the children of Israel. Samuel is also the first in the order of prophets whose role was to speak to the people the words and will of God. God actually defined the role and function of prophets, when in Deuteronomy 18:18–19, He, through Moses, said, *"I will raise up a prophet from among their countrymen like you, and I will put my words in his mouth, and he shall speak to them all*

that I command him. And it shall come about that who-
ever will not listen to my words which he shall speak in My
name, I Myself will require it of him."

Prophets are people who foretell the future. Their
foretelling are not predictions, but God saying what
will happen in the future. The final prophet was Jesus
himself. Some people speak of Jesus in the same vein as
the prophet Mohammed of Islam; the difference being
that Jesus was more than a prophet. He was the son
of God, even God himself in human form. We see in
Samuel a foreshadowing of Jesus because Samuel was
a prophet, a priest, and an erstwhile ruler as the last of
the judge leaders of Israel.

The story of Samuel is another unique story of
God's direct intervention in someone's life to accomplish His ultimate will, that of grace and mercy. Samuel
was raised in the temple by the High Priest Eli. He had
been dedicated to the Lord by his mother, Hannah,
who delivered Samuel to Eli after he was weaned. God
spoke to Samuel when he was an adolescent and told
him that Eli had been negligent in correcting his two
corrupt sons, Phineas and Hophni, and, therefore,
would be eliminating Eli and his sons. The sons had
been abusing their roles in the temple by taking the
choice cuts of sacrificial meats and forcing sex with
women who came to the temple to worship. 1 Samuel
4:19 says, *"Samuel grew and the Lord was with him and*

let none of his words fail." That is the proof of a true prophet as was discussed earlier.

Now as I said previously, Israel wanted a king. They wanted a ruler they could see and touch and who would listen to them. So the elders of Israel came to Samuel and told him, "The people want you to appoint a king for us to judge us like all the other nations." Samuel prayed, and Lord said to Samuel, "*Listen to the voice of the people in regard to all that they say to you, for they have not rejected you, but they have rejected Me from being king over them. You shall solemnly warn them and tell them of the procedure of the king who will reign over them*" (1 Samuel 8:7).

Samuel explained to the people the negative aspects of having a king, including the king's power to impose onerous laws, tax them, draft them for hard labor, and take the best of their fields for the kingdom, etc. Nevertheless, the people insisted on having a king. But there were great positive aspects too. When they had been led by Moses and Joshua, they were a united people. After 385 years of judges and lots of tribe-centered battles, the twelve tribes of Israel could be unified under a single leader.

God told Samuel to appoint a king and identified Saul from the tribe of Benjamin as the one to be anointed. When Saul took over the kingdom of Israel, he fought against all his enemies on every side, against Moab, the sons of Ammon, Edom, the kings of Zobah, and the Philistines. Wherever he turned, he inflicted punishment. He acted valiantly and defeated the Amalekites, and he delivered Israel from the hands of those who plundered them.

Samuel admonished the people to fear the Lord and serve Him in truth with all their heart. In 1 Samuel 12, Samuel said, *"But if you shall do wickedly, both you and your king shall be swept away."*

This is a verse for us today and should be looked at from a positive viewpoint. Restated, it says that if we please God in our daily actions and thoughts, i.e., being Christlike, we are in for a blessing. Our king is Jesus Christ, who reigns forever.

After a series of events in which Saul was disobedient to the rules God gave him through Samuel, Samuel declared to Saul that God would remove him from his kingship. God told Samuel to find Saul's replacement from the sons of Jesse, a Bethlehemite. Being afraid of Saul, Samuel did this secretly and anointed David, Jesse's youngest son, to succeed Saul as king.

When Saul made an unauthorized sacrifice in direct disobedience to God, Samuel said, *"Has the Lord so much delight in burnt offerings and sacrifices as in obeying the voice of the Lord? Behold, to obey is better than sacrifice. Because you have rejected the word of the Lord, He has also rejected you from being king. The Lord has torn the kingdom of Israel from you today, and has given it to your neighbor, who is better than you"* (1 Samuel 15:22).

Obedience. Not sacrifice, not tithes, not offerings. God wants obedience from us. He gave us the rules for our relationship with Him and with our neighbors, our fellow man. As it says in 1 John 5:3, *"For this is the love of God, that we keep His commandments, and His commandments are not burdensome."* God's laws are simple and straightforward. We do not have to worry about memorizing the Ten Commandments. We just have to know two of them: love the Lord your God with all your heart, soul, and mind, and love your neighbor as yourself. If we love God with all our hearts, we will not worship idols, such as money or fame. If we love our neighbor as ourself, we will not murder, lie, steal, commit adultery, gossip, etc. However, it is not that simple in practice as we know.

One of the most well-known stories in the Bible comes from 1 Samuel and is the story of David and Goliath. The Philistines and Israelites were arrayed for battle, and the Philistines had a giant, over nine feet tall, covered with armor. He daily taunted the Israelites. God used David to slay the giant, Goliath, with only a stone and a sling.

I want to point out here an important fact, one which has been ignored in the telling of this story in modern times. We have been told from childhood that

David was a young lad when he went out to fight the giant Goliath. Remember the song:

> Only a boy named David, only a little
>   sling,
> only a boy named David, but he could
>   pray and sing.
> Only a boy named David, only a rip-
>   pling brook,
> only a boy named David, but five lit-
>   tle stones he took. And one little
>   stone went in the sling, and the
>   sling went round and round,
> and one little stone went in the sling
>   and the sling went round and
>   round,
> and round and round and round and
>   round, and round and round and
>   round.
> And one little stone went up in the
>   air, and the giant came tumbling
>   down.

Here is the important fact of this story: David was not a young boy when he fought Goliath. 1 Samuel 16:18 says, "*David was a mighty man of valor, a warrior, one prudent in speech and a handsome man, and the Lord was with him.*" That was the key to victory, the Lord was with him. David was no match for this giant veteran of war. David's faith in the Almighty was, in reality, his weapon. God guided the stone with the force needed to the exact spot, the giant's forehead unprotected by armor, to knock Goliath out and allow David to cut off his head with Goliath's own sword. The Israelites then routed the Philistine army that day, but the war was not over.

1 Samuel is a very exciting book to read and tells how Saul chased David around Israel trying to kill him, even though David is blameless of trying to harm Saul or usurp his kingdom. David recognized that Saul was the Lord's anointed and, therefore, refused to fight back. Eventually, the Philistines killed Saul in battle, and David became king in his place. 1 Samuel ends with Saul's and his son's deaths.

The book of 2 Samuel is primarily a biography of David after he became king. It details his triumphs over all his enemies, his transgressions, and the trouble he experienced as a result of his sins. David is initially made king over Judah, the southernmost kingdom, after Saul's death. He defeats the army of Israel, who had made one of the surviving sons of Saul king and thereby unites Israel and Judah.

David is a type of Christ despite his sins. The story of David and his triumphs is exciting, but there is also a sad side to it. God called David a man after His own heart before he was made king. Then David committed adultery with the wife of one of his soldiers who was away on the battlefield; and subsequently, he had the husband, Uriah, killed in battle to hide his sin.

This sad episode discloses the weakness of many men, lust. David could have had most any woman he desired since he was king, but taking another man's wife was and is clearly out of bounds and a sin. But that was not all David was guilty of. He committed murder, another grievous sin, by having his army commander bring about Uriah's death to hide his sin of adultery with Uriah's wife.

Was David still a man after God's own heart after his sins? God hates sin. Well, who among us has not sinned, and yet we can be right with God when we repent? The answer is true remorseful repentance. Have you ever been sorry for any sin you committed? I have. But being remorseful is not enough. One has to go before God in humility of spirit and confess that sin to God. Remember the verse in Lamentations, *"His mercies are new every morning."* God's door is open 24-7. He wants every sinner, no matter how vile, to come to Him and confess his sins so that his or her relationship with God can be restored. However, confession is empty if there is no repentance. Repentance means to turn away from our sins into a new path of righteousness. If one continues in that sin, the relationship with God remains broken. In 1 John 1:9, God says, *"If we confess our sins, he is faithful and just to forgive our sins and to cleanse us from all unrighteousness."* That is love.

When the priest and prophet Nathan confronted David with his sin, David saw how awful it was. David went to his knees and confessed. There are some Psalms written by David that express his true remorse for his sins, one of note being Psalms 51:

> Be gracious unto me O God, according to thy loving kindness; according to the greatness of thy compassion blot out my transgressions. Wash me thoroughly from my iniquity, and cleanse me from my sin. For I know my transgressions, and my sin is ever before me. Against Thee, Thee only, I have sinned… Create in me a clean heart, O God, and renew a steadfast spirit within me. Do not cast me away from Thy presence, and do not take the Holy Spirit from me.

David repented and turned his life into one that was the model for all future kings, and yes, for us too. During his reign, there is no record of idol worship; in his Psalms, he constantly proclaimed how beautiful were the statutes of the Lord.

But there are consequences of sin, and Nathan prophesied of the events that would happen to David and his family. There was incest within David's house, although it was actually a rape of David's daughter, Tamar, by his firstborn son, Amnon. Later, Tamar's brother Absolom had Amnon killed. Then much later, when Absolom tried to usurp the throne from David, he was killed by David's army commander, Joab.

The book of 2 Samuel ends with David's death of old age, even though he was only seventy years old. His many years of battle and the pressures of being king may have contributed to his death, nor can it be ruled out that God decided it was time for David's son Solomon to replace him as king.

CHAPTER 7

1 AND 2 KINGS

The mostly likely author for 1 and 2 Kings was Jeremiah. We, therefore, have a better understanding of where Jeremiah fits in the narrative of the kings after the kingdom of Israel and Judah is divided into the northern and southern kingdoms. Jeremiah was a prophet in Judah when first Aram, then Assyria and Babylon began their attempts to capture it.

In 1 Kings, Solomon is established as king, and he quickly eliminates those who might be usurpers of, or dangerous, to his throne. He had his half-brother Adonijah and Joab, David's army commander, killed. He banished Abiathar the priest rather than having him killed because he had supported Adonijah in his quest for the throne after David.

Solomon is generally known for three things: his wisdom, his wealth, and his many wives. Shortly after Solomon was anointed king, he prayed to the Lord for wisdom and understanding "to rightly rule over so great a people." God told Solomon that because he had not asked for riches for himself, He would give him a wise and discerning heart. Then God told him that he would also give him riches and honor. Solomon was known as one of the richest men who ever lived.

Solomon's wisdom is exemplified by the story of the two women who both claimed the same baby as theirs after the non-mother had lain on her child in her sleep and killed it. Solomon asked that a sword be brought, and he would divide the baby and give each woman half. The real mother spoke to Solomon and said, "By no means harm the child. Give it to the other woman." By that, Solomon knew who the real mother was and gave her the baby.

In Solomon's early years of reign, he can be compared with Christ in his wisdom, and his fame and glory foreshadow Jesus in His kingdom. But Solomon sinned when he made alliances with other countries by marrying women from those countries' royalties. He had seven hundred wives and three hundred concubines. These wives turned his heart away from the Lord in his later years, and he allowed their pagan religions to be practiced in Israel. Because of this, God tore the kingdom from Solomon's son after Solomon's death. However, Rehoboam, Solomon's son, was allowed to keep the tribe of Judah to reign over.

Rehoboam reigned seventeen years as king of Judah, but apparently, he had not understood the rea-

— ✧ 80 ✧ —

son Solomon lost the territories of ten tribes because Judah continued doing evil in the sight of the Lord.

God did not abandon the people of the northern kingdom; they were still Jews, his chosen people. However, 2 Kings declares that every king who ascended to the throne in Israel did evil in the sight of the Lord. In Judah, the kings were only a little better with only five of twenty kings being classified as good their entire reign. Because of their evil ways, God allowed Assyria to capture and exile the Israelites (Northern Kingdom) in 722 BC and the Babylonians to capture and exile the Judeans about 150 years later in 586 BC.

In Babylon, the Jews remained isolated from the Babylonians; and when they returned to Judah seventy years later, they had remained a pure Jewish race. The Israelites who were exiled to Assyria never returned. They intermarried with the Assyrians, both in Assyria and Samaria, thereby despoiling their race. Six hundred years later, when Jesus walked the earth, the Judeans would not have anything to do with Samaritans because they were no longer considered Jews by the Judeans. The Jewish religion was reestablished in Samaria, but there was no friendly contact between the two peoples. Jesus was from the Galilean district north of Samaria, where there were orthodox Jews. When Jews traveled between Judah and Galilee, they would cross over the Jordan River to the east to make the trip so that they would not pass through Samaria. Jesus, however, took the direct route and engaged the Samaritan woman at the well as told in John 4 and told her of the living water that was available through Him.

One of the most notable stories of the Bible involves Ahab, the eighth king of Israel (Northern Kingdom). Although it appears that Ahab had good intentions of being a godly king, he made a grave mistake by marrying Jezebel, daughter of the king of the Sidonians, and went to serve and worship Baal there. Jezebel pleased Ahab, so Ahab did what Jezebel wanted, and that was to turn Israel into a nation that worshipped Baal as their god. Jezebel waged a campaign against and began killing the prophets and priests of Israel. Hundreds were saved by hiding in caves. God sent his prophet, Elijah, to Ahab to tell him there would be no rain for three years. Elijah then hid himself for those three years, during which time the Lord provided for him by a number of miracles. Elijah is a foreshadowing of Jesus in performing two miracles: providing a destitute woman with food for many days and also raising her son from the dead as Jesus raised Lazarus from the dead.

At the end of three years, the Lord sent Elijah to Ahab. Elijah told King Ahab to gather the 450 prophets of Baal and 400 prophets of the Asherah at Mount Carmel. When they had gathered, Elijah proposed to the people a contest to see who was God. He proposed that he and they would each build a wooden altar and offer an ox on it, and the god who answered by fire, He was God. And all the people answered and said that was a good idea.

The prophets of Baal called and pleaded to their god, but he did not answer. Then Elijah had the people pour water on his offering and on the wood and fill a trench surrounding the altar with water. He then called for God to bring fire and consume the altar. Then the fire of the Lord fell and consumed the offering, along with the wood, the stones, and the water that was in the trench. And when all the people saw it, they fell on their faces and declared, "The Lord, He is God!" Then Elijah said to them, "Seize the prophets of Baal. Do not let one of them escape." So they seized them, and Elijah brought them down to the brook Kishon and slew all of them there.

Elijah then told Ahab to go home because it was going to rain. In a little while, the sky grew black with clouds and wind, and there was a heavy rain. Ahab told Jezebel all that Elijah had done and how he had killed all the Baal prophets with the sword. Then Jezebel sent a messenger to Elijah, saying, "You are a dead man." So Elijah went to Beersheba in Judah to hide. When Elijah found himself at Mount Sinai, God met him there and told him to return and anoint a new king in Aram, present-day Syria, who was warring with Israel, and to anoint Elisha to replace him as prophet.

Jezebel was an evil woman. When Ahab wanted to acquire Naboth's vineyard, which was particularly productive and near Ahab's castle and Naboth would not give it or trade it to Ahab, Jezebel had Naboth killed under false charges and gave the vineyard to Ahab.

Then the Lord told Elijah to go down to meet Ahab, King of Israel, in Samaria, where Ahab had gone to take possession of Naboth's vineyard. Elijah told Ahab that because he had sold himself to do evil in the sight of the Lord, the Lord would bring evil upon him and sweep him away. He also said that the dogs would eat Jezebel in the streets of Jezreel. When Ahab heard these words from Elijah, he tore his clothes and put on sackcloth and fasted and went about despondently. God then told Elijah that because Ahab had humbled himself and truly shown repentance, he would not bring evil against Ahab in his days, but He would remove Ahab and his heirs in his son's days. Ahab was killed in battle soon thereafter, and his son, Joram, took the throne. Ahab's confession of his sins caused God to delay judgment.

About this time, God sent a chariot of fire to get Elijah and take him to heaven. Elijah was replaced as Israel's prophet by Elisha. The Lord told Elisha to anoint Jehu, who was not of the house of Ahab, to be king of Israel. Jehu was actually a grandson of Jehoshaphat, a former king of Judah and ancestor of Jesus.

When Jehu rode into the palace at Jezreel to take the throne, Jezebel spoke in derision to him from an upper floor. Jehu commanded that she be thrown out the window, the first known case of defenestration. She was thrown out of the upper-floor window by her eunuchs and was trampled by Jehu's horse, after which she was eaten by dogs; there was nothing left of her to bury.

Jezebel's influence was also felt in Judah as her daughter, Athaliah, executed a coup and killed all of the royal line of David, with the exception of the baby, Josiah, whom his nurse saved and hid, thus preserving the house of David's eternal reign and the ancestry of Jesus.

The story of Elisha and his ministry is similar to that of Elijah. Notably, as Jesus would do in the future in multiplying five loaves and two fishes to feed five thousand people, Elisha multiplied a few loaves of bread for a hundred men so that they ate their fill, and he healed a man of leprosy. Elisha would also live among the people for which he was the priest and preach a message of hope and grace just as Jesus did centuries later.

Another key figure in 2 Kings is the king Mannaseh. He was the son of Hezekiah, who was one of the so-called good kings who reigned in Judah. Mannaseh was the evilest of all the kings of Judah and destroyed all the advances Hezekiah had made to get Judah back on track to worshipping Yahweh. Mannaseh was in the genealogical line of Jesus. After Mannaseh died, his son, Josiah, became king at the age of eight and spent his years returning Judah to worship of Yahweh and destroying all the idols emplaced by Mannaseh all over Judah and in the temple in Jerusalem.

CHAPTER 8

1 AND 2 CHRONICLES

The books of 1 and 2 Chronicles covers the same period as 2 Samuel and 1 and 2 Kings. In 2 Samuel, we have the account of David's sin with Bathsheba and, in the remainder of the book, David's suffering through the results of that sin as prophesied by Nathan the prophet. In 1 Chronicles, the first nine chapters covers genealogies of Israel's sons, and in particular, the genealogy of David from Adam to Zerubbabel. It is widely accepted that Ezra the Priest wrote 1 and 2 Chronicles since the genealogy extended to Zerubbabel, who lived during the time of Ezra when the Jews were exiled in Babylon. It is quite possible that Ezra wrote the Chronicles to remind the newly returned Jews to Judah from their seventy-year exile of their heritage.

Chapter 10 of 1 Chronicles tells of the end of the house of Saul, and chapters 11–29 are a history of David's forty-year reign over Israel and Judah, without the mention of David's sin of adultery and murder and their resulting consequences on him and his family. That history includes his victories over all those countries surrounding Israel and his committing the sin of numbering all the tribes of Israel, which God specifically forbade. God then punished David, which led to David's acquiring the site of Orman's threshing floor on which David built an altar and offered sacrifices and repented before God. This site later became the site where Solomon built the first temple to replace the tabernacle (2 Chronicles 3:1).

David has already been recognized as a type of Christ in 1 Samuel as a shepherd, a savior in his victory over Goliath and the Philistines, and an eternal king. He was a great king over all of Israel and Judah and never allowed the Israelites to worship anyone but Yahweh.

Chapters 1 to 9 of 2 Chronicles covers the reign of Solomon over Israel and Judah. It covers the construction of the temple and all its contents and Solomon's great wealth. Solomon's sermon and prayer of dedication of the newly built temple are marvelous passages in chapter 6, and having read them, one has to wonder how Solomon fell from grace with God and had the kingdom torn from him. 2 Chronicles does not mention the sins of his later years, where he allowed worship of foreign gods in Israel when his foreign wives turned his heart away from God.

In chapter 10, the kingdom is divided, and Solomon's son, Rehoboam, is left with only the kingdom of Judah, which was inhabited by the tribes of Judah and Benjamin. The remainder of 2 Chronicles enumerates the rest of the seventeen kings of Judah but spends more time on the five good kings, those who restored the temple and kept to the example of David. Hezekiah was one of the kings who did right in the sight of the Lord. He succeeded Ahaz, a particularly evil king who desecrated the temple. God allowed the King of Aram to defeat Ahaz and carry some captives from Judah to Damascus. When Hezekiah became king, he ordered the cleansing of the temple and led Judah in turning their hearts to the Lord. He fortified the cities of Judah. When Sennacherib, the king of Assyria, came to invade Judah with an army of 185,000 thousand soldiers, King Hezekiah and the prophet Isaiah prayed to God for deliverance, and the Lord defeated his army without the Judeans lifting an arm against them. About this time, Isaiah prophesied that a future king named Cyrus would decree that Jerusalem would be raised from its ruins (Isaiah 44:26–28). This was over 150 years before Cyrus became king of Persia.

Of the remaining kings of Judah, only Josiah was declared to be true to the Lord, and he reigned forty years until he was killed by the king of Egypt. Neco, King of Egypt, installed Josiah's sons as kings, and they did evil in the sight of the Lord. Nebuchadnezzar,

King of Babylon, then captured Jerusalem during Jehoiakim's reign and began taking Jews to Babylon. He put Zedekiah on the throne of Judah. Zedekiah was the last of the kings of Judah and did evil in the sight of the Lord. He also rebelled against the king of Babylon, who, in response, sacked Jerusalem, burned the temple and carried away its treasures, and took away the inhabitants of Judah to Babylon.

It is instructive to note that the prophet Jeremiah is first mentioned in 2 Chronicles during the reign of Josiah. In Jeremiah 25:1–12, Jeremiah speaks to King Jehoiakim and said he had been warning the kings of Judah of coming judgment for twenty-three years, and that Judah would be exiled to Babylon for seventy years.

CHAPTER 9

EZRA, NEHEMIAH, AND ESTHER

When Ezra wrote 1 and 2 Chronicles, Ezra, and perhaps part of Nehemiah, was in Jerusalem, having traveled from Babylon in the seventh year of the Persian King Ahasuerus (Ezra 7:7), which would be in the year 479 BC, 107 years after Jerusalem was sacked and Jewish prisoners taken to Babylon.

The book of *Ezra* tells of the return to Judah of many Jews after they had been in exile for seventy years. In 539 BC, Persia, under King Cyrus, overthrew Babylon. The next year, he decreed that a temple would be built in Jerusalem for the God of heaven and that all Jews who desired could go to Jerusalem to assist in its building. Nearly fifty thousand Jews returned to Jerusalem and Judah in 538 BC, led by Zerubbabel, who was in the genealogical line of Jesus. Zerubbabel was the great grandson of the last good king of Judah, Josiah.

Zerubbabel began building the temple in the second year after their arrival in Jerusalem. There was resistance by the local people to this work, as well as from the governor of the entire Trans-Euphrates area (all the area controlled by the Persians west of the Euphrates River). The governor, Tattenai, did not want Jerusalem and the temple rebuilt, so he wrote to King Darius and asked if Cyrus had actually given the decree to build a temple in Jerusalem. After a search of the records, Darius sent a letter to Tattenai confirming the decree by Cyrus and furthermore instructed Tattenai to give resources and all assistance to the Jews to complete the temple.

The passage in Ezra 4 concerning the letter to Artaxerxes apparently is misplaced because it has nothing to do with building the temple, but with the building of the wall around Jerusalem, which actually occurred during the reign of Artaxerxes sixty-seven or sixty-eight years later by Nehemiah.

The book of Nehemiah relates Nehemiah's close relationship with King Artaxerxes, being his winetaster. Nehemiah asked for and got letters from Artaxerxes, allowing him safe passage to Jerusalem to rebuild the walls of Jerusalem. This occurred in the twentieth year of Artaxerxes's reign or in the year 444 BC. Historically, and for perspective, the Greeks had defeated an invading army from Persia under King Darius I at the battle of Marathon in 490 BC.

Nehemiah arrived in Jerusalem and immediately set about rebuilding the walls around Jerusalem. Even though Nehemiah and the workers were threatened, the walls were completed in fifty-two days. Christ is exemplified by Nehemiah in that he gave up his position of power under Artaxerxes and went to work with his people in Jerusalem. Nehemiah also did a lot of praying for guidance for the job of restoration he had come to do. Nehemiah then had Ezra read the law to the people and led the Jews in a revival to return to obeying God, to include requiring those who had married foreign wives to give them up.

The book of *Esther* is interesting in many respects. It does not contain the name of God, yet God's hand in the preservation of his people is quite evident. This book contains the history of the first, as far as we know, attempt at a holocaust, the complete elimination of the Jews throughout the entire Persian Empire from India to Ethiopia, which included Israel and Judah.

Esther is a Jewish virgin who has been swept up into the king's harem because of her great beauty. She became such a favorite of King Ahasuerus that he made her queen. Haman, a man of some prominence in the king's court, hated the Jew Mordecai and deluded the king into believing that the Jews were a dangerous and rebellious people and should be eliminated. The king agreed and, by decree, gave Haman the authority to destroy them. Haman had a very tall gallows built on which he planned to hang Mordecai. Mordecai, Esther's stepfather, convinced Esther that she was in the king's court for the express purpose of saving the Jews from annihilation. Esther hatched an incredible plan whereby the king, who could not by law recall his decree, issued another decree, which allowed the Jews to protect themselves on the day chosen for the peoples of the empire to rise up and kill the Jews in their cities and provinces. When Haman was exposed to the king by Esther, the king had Haman hanged on the very gallows that Haman had built for Mordecai.

Esther was a type of Christ who, like Joseph many centuries before, had been appointed by God to preserve the Jewish people in Egypt. Just as the Jews have celebrated the Passover when they were delivered from Egypt, they also celebrate Purim, which is the day the Jews were appointed to die in the Persian Empire but were delivered by Esther's heroics. Esther was a heroine because she placed her own life in jeopardy to get an audience with the king when he had not summoned her into his court, which was punishable by death. The king saw her and was favorably disposed toward her and invited her to come to his throne. She informed him of the fraudulent conspiracy against the Jews by Haman. As Jesus is our advocate with God, Esther was an advocate for the Jews of the Persian Empire with the king of Persia.

CHAPTER 10

JOB

This is the big exception to the thesis of this book, that Jesus is characterized or his genealogy is furthered or ensured in most of the books of the Bible. Job was supposedly the first book of the Bible written, but its author is unknown. I believe that the Bible is the inspired Word of God, but that does not make the story of Job a true one. I believe the story of Job is allegorical or a type of parable. Let's discuss that.

Jesus told parables to express a point to his disciples or to the skeptics, notably the Pharisees. The fact that Job is mentioned in the books of Ezekiel and James does not make it a true story. It only means that Ezekiel and James had read the story, which apparently was a part of the scriptures in their times.

Job was an upright man who lived in Uz. He was a very rich man, owning seven thousand sheep, three thousand camels, and five hundred female donkeys. This story supposedly took place before the time of

Abraham and perhaps occurred in Southeast Arabia, although no one really knows where Uz was. With those holdings, he was known as the richest man in the east. He had seven sons and three daughters, each of whom had their own families. It is amazing that calamity struck and wiped out all of Job's possessions and families within a matter of hours, all in one day. Fire came from heaven and consumed seven thousand sheep and all the shepherds. Sabeans attacked and took his oxen and donkeys and slew the servants with them. The Chaldeans came and took his three thousand camels and slew the servants with them. A great wind came and flattened the house where all his sons and daughters and grandchildren were having a big party and killed them all.

Call me skeptical, but this story is hard to swallow, but that is what it is, a story. And it has a purpose, just as Jesus's parables had a purpose. A lot of people have asked the question, "Why do bad things happen to good people?" The book of Job does not address this question. Rather, it is a story of faith and trust.

Satan posits to God that the only reason people follow Him is for the good treatment God gives them and were He to take those things away, they would curse God to His face. To disabuse Satan of his accusation, God has to let Satan carry out his plan to afflict Job, the most upright man existing at the moment, by destroying his vast possessions and putting unbearable illnesses upon him. Satan thinks Job will reject God when this happens. Job's three best friends come to console, commiserate, and accuse him. But Job stays faithful throughout the ordeal. He argues with God, questions God's intentions, finally admits he is a sinner, and God restores him.

So there really is a message of salvation in this story. When we are repentant, God will restore us. God doesn't afflict us, Satan does. God allows things to happen for His purposes.

CHAPTER II

PSALMS, PROVERBS, ECCLESIASTES, AND SONG OF SOLOMON

Psalms

The word Psalm means song. The Psalms were actually sung in Jewish worship. How much more worshipful could one be to sing these songs of praise to our Creator. Seventy-five of the psalms are attributable to David, one to Moses, and two to Solomon. Many were written by choir directors appointed to lead the musicians in singing praise in the temple after the time of David and before the fifth century BC. Fifty Psalms were written by authors unknown.

I have many wonderful childhood memories of reciting Psalms 23 daily in the public elementary school in Cottondale, Florida, and learning in Vacation Bible School in my little country church, in Alford, Florida, "*Thy Word is a lamp to my feet, a light to my path always*" (Psalms 119:105). We also learned Psalms 19:14, "*Let the words of my mouth and the meditation of my heart be acceptable in thy sight, O Lord, my rock and my Redeemer.*" These are wonderful verses to use as daily devotional prayers. Psalms is a great place to begin each day with words of praise and thanksgiving to God.

There are twenty-two prophecies of Jesus in fifteen Psalms, including eleven Davidic Psalms. Seven of these prophecies pertain to Jesus's crucifixion. For example, Psalms 22:16 and 18 prophesies, "*They pierced my hands and my feet. They divided my garments among them, and for my clothing they cast lots.*" This prophesy is fulfilled in John 20:25 and 27 and Matthew 27:35.

Psalms 91, author unknown, is a wonderful confession of how God is a shelter to us. He is our refuge and fortress. He will cover us with his pinions. It says that the days of our lives are seventy years or, if due to strength, eighty years, and the pride of our years are labor and sorrow. Psalms 90 is the only psalm written by Moses. Moses says in verse 12, "*Teach us to number our days, that we may present to God a heart of wisdom.*" We are to spend the days of our lives in seeking wisdom. Proverbs 2:1–6 says we are to "seek for wisdom as for a hidden treasure. Then we will discern the fear of the Lord, and discover the knowledge of God."

Proverbs

Proverbs is the book of wise sayings. Solomon is most well-known for his wisdom, and 1 Kings 4:32 says that Solomon spoke three thousand proverbs and wrote 1,005 songs. The book of Proverbs contains around eight hundred of his proverbs. Solomon is thought to be the author of some twenty-six of the thirty-one chapters of Proverbs.

Proverbs 4 says to take heed in the instruction of fathers, for fathers give sound teachings. This biblical fatherly instruction is *"Acquire wisdom. Acquire understanding."* and *"The beginning of wisdom is 'Acquire wisdom."* The primary instruction of the father is to get wisdom. And what better wisdom to get than that of Jesus Christ. In Colossians 2:3, it says that in Christ are hidden all the treasures of wisdom and knowledge. Proverbs 3:13 says, *"How blessed is the man who finds wisdom, and the man who gains understanding."*

Proverbs has good advice for all ages and endeavors. It speaks on adultery, faithfulness to one's spouse, relationships with others, and using good business sense, such as not becoming surety for others. For example, you should never cosign a loan, because if your cosigner defaults, you will be required to repay the loan. The book of Proverbs has thirty-one chapters, which makes it a good source of daily devotions, providing a chapter for each day of a month.

Ecclesiastes

The writer or speaker of Ecclesiastes is called the preacher. Chapter 1 verses 1 and 12 tells us that the preacher is the son of David and that the preacher was the king of Israel in Jerusalem, so we know that the writer of this book is Solomon. Proverbs 25:2 says, "*It is the glory of Kings to search out a matter.*" Solomon, king and known as the wisest person ever, searched out all matters that came to his attention. Unfortunately, Solomon's curiosities went so far as to want anything that added to his pleasures, including obtaining hundreds of wives and concubines. After experiencing everything life could offer him and saying that there was nothing new under the sun, he said, "Vanity of vanities, all is vanity." He realized that no matter what occurs in one's life, in the end, we all return to the dust of the earth and our spirit returns to God.

Even though Solomon was a purveyor of wisdom, his wisdom failed him when he married foreign wives and they turned his heart away from God. He did not remember the early wisdom given by a father: "Keep my commandments and live." That was God's commandment, "Do not marry foreign wives." The penultimate verse in Ecclesiastes is "*The conclusion is, when all has been heard, fear God and keep his commandments, because this applies to every person.*"

Perhaps Solomon was writing to express his regrets for his folly and time spent in carnality. Other than that, we cannot find where Solomon ever repented before God for his sins of lust and idolatry and leading his kingdom astray.

As was discussed in Proverbs, wisdom is found in Jesus Christ. In chapter 11 verse 9, Solomon said if we follow the impulses of our heart and desires of our eyes, God will judge us for all these things. Too bad he did not adhere to his own wisdom.

Song of Solomon

This is an allegorical love song or poem thought to have been written by Solomon as the name Solomon occurs several times in it. There are fifteen geographic locations mentioned in the poem from the far north of Israel to the southern border. Metaphorically, with those location disclosures and other descriptions of the land and monuments, the poem would seem to be describing God's love for Israel, His chosen people. The descriptions of the wooing of a beautiful maiden could describe God's wooing of his people (His bride) to cling to Him only and love only Him and not turn to idols. We may contrast this with the New Testament description of the church (believers) as the bride of Christ.

The supposed words of Solomon, the prospective bridegroom and lover, could, in fact, be directed to a special woman of his harem, which is numbered at sixty queens and eighty concubines (chapter 6 verse 9) at the time the poem was written. This could be the case as when we look back at Esther, who was the special one that King Ahasuerus chose from his harem.

CHAPTER 12

THE BOOKS OF THE MAJOR PROPHETS: ISAIAH, JEREMIAH, LAMENTATIONS, EZEKIEL, DANIEL

When the book of 2 Kings concludes, the major historical events of the Old Testament have been enumerated. The kingdom of Israel had been divided into northern and southern kingdoms. The northern kingdom, consisting of ten tribes of Israel, is called Israel, and the southern kingdom, consisting of the tribes of Benjamin and Judah, is called Judah. Israel was conquered by Assyria, and its people carried off to places east in 722 BC. In 586 BC, Judah was conquered, and many of its people carried off to Babylon. During the centuries before their defeat by the Assyrians and Babylonians, God sent prophets to the kings of the two kingdoms, warning them that they must amend their wicked ways or face dire consequences, specifically the overthrow of Samaria and Judah and the destruction of Jerusalem. Isaiah and Jeremiah were two of these prophets. Ezekiel ministered to the Jews exiled in Babylon at the same time Jeremiah ministered to the Jews in Judah.

When studying the history of Jews after the time of David, Israel under Solomon became a very rich country. Solomon was a wise and shrewd businessman who brokered all kinds of goods from livestock to everything that traversed the silk road which ran through Israel. Israel controlled the passage of goods coming to and going from Egypt to Damascus, the capital of Aram, in particular. It may have been for that reason that first Aram, then Assyria and Babylon, warred against Israel to receive the riches that Israel was gaining from controlling the trade routes. It follows that because of the riches they enjoyed, the Israelites turned away from God and did as every man thought was right in his own eyes. Hence, God sent prophets to urge his people to get back on track, reject idolatry, and return to obeying Him.

Isaiah

Perhaps the most recognized passage in Isaiah is chapter 53, which describes the future Jesus who will atone for the sins of the world and is the basis for the composer Handel's Oratorio, "Messiah." Isaiah is known for his prophesies. One Bible scholar has listed

121 prophetic verses in Isaiah pertaining to the future Messiah.

Isaiah was a prophet in Judah during the reign of four kings over a period of sixty years. Isaiah was well-educated and a keen observer of the wars being waged against the northern kingdom by the king of Aram and subsequently by Assyria. He was ministering to both Israel and Judah at the same time, which allowed him to be knowledgeable of Aram's and Assyria's wars with Israel. Isaiah's message to both countries was "Turn to God. Only He can save you."

Isaiah began his ministry during the last years of Azariah's (Uzziah) reign. Uzziah was one of the good kings of Judah. Talmudic tradition holds that Isaiah was Azariah's first cousin, thereby giving him access to the royal courts, putting him in position to be a priestly advisor to the king and his successor son (Jotham) and grandson (Ahaz), his first cousins once and twice removed. Isaiah encouraged Ahaz to turn his heart and people back to God and be saved from the Arameans. Ahaz turned against God and worshipped the gods of the Assyrians whom he had paid from the treasures of the temple to fight against the Arameans. Assyria then defeated the Arameans, which also ended the Arameans siege of the northern kingdom for a while. However, the king of Assyria demanded tribute from Israel to keep the Assyrians from invading them. When Israel's king, Hoshea, tried to get the king of

Egypt to help him throw off the Assyrians, Assyrian King Shalmaneser found out about the conspiracy and invaded and defeated Israel and transported the majority of the Israelites to Assyria.

Isaiah tried to convince Ahaz, even said to Ahaz, "Ask a sign from the Lord. Test the Lord." But Ahaz had turned away and would not be persuaded to trust in Yahweh, the God of the Jews. Ahaz died of an unstated cause when he was thirty-eight years old, and Hezekiah, his son, took over kingship of Judah. He was not buried among the kings of Judah, so one might conclude that the people overthrew him because of the evil he did.

Hezekiah was a good king and, having seen the evil of his father, knew he must lead Judah in a different direction, back to God. He became a frequent listener to Isaiah, and when the Assyrian King Sennacherib surrounded Jerusalem with 185,000 soldiers, Isaiah prayed to God for deliverance, and God sent an angel to destroy his entire army at night.

Later, Hezekiah became very sick, and the king of Babylon sent an envoy to visit Hezekiah and bring him a gift in his illness. Hezekiah foolishly showed the envoy all the treasures of the kingdom. 2 Kings 20:14–18 gives this account: *"Then Isaiah the prophet came to King Hezekiah and said to him, 'What did these men say, and from where have they come to you?' And Hezekiah said, 'They have come from a far country, from*

Babylon.' And he said, 'What have they seen in your house? So, Hezekiah answered, 'They have seen all that is in my house; there is nothing among my treasure that I have not shown them.' Then Isaiah said to Hezekiah, 'Hear the word of the Lord. Behold, the days are coming when all that is in your house, and all that your fathers have laid up in store to this day shall be carried to Babylon; nothing shall be left,' says the Lord. And some of your sons who shall issue from you, whom you shall beget, shall be taken away, and they should become officials in the palace of the king of Babylon'."

After Hezekiah died, his son Mannaseh became king. He was perhaps the most wicked of all the kings of Judah. He quickly grew tired of Isaiah and, according to Talmudic tradition, had Isaiah killed. At the end of Manasseh's life, he repented and God restored him. God is merciful.

Jeremiah

Jeremiah is known as the weeping prophet. He ministered to Judah for forty years immediately prior to Judah's captivity and exile by the Babylonians. His message to Judah was very similar to that of Isaiah about one hundred years earlier: turn back to God or suffer calamitous consequences. As in Isaiah's time, Judeans worshipped and prayed to God insincerely, and God rejected their false worship. Jeremiah warned the Judeans that they cannot just say the words "the temple of the Lord, the temple of the Lord, the temple of the Lord" and expect God to hear and bless them (Jeremiah 7:4). They must put words into actions and love their neighbors, not oppress the aliens, widows, and orphans. They were also burning incense and sacrificing to other gods, covering all bases as it were.

Jeremiah preached twelve sermons to Judah in which he laid out the message from God that Judah had abandoned God and gone after other gods. Jeremiah could only weep as he pleaded with the people to acknowledge their sin and return to the God that had brought them out of Egypt and to this Promised Land. In Jeremiah, we see a foreshadowing of Jesus as Jeremiah wept for Jerusalem, seeing its impending destruction by Babylon. Jesus wept for Jerusalem, knowing that not many years later, it would be destroyed and looted by Rome.

Around 620 BC, Jeremiah became a prophet in the court of Josiah, the last "good" king. In 612 BC, Babylon captured the impregnable city of Nineveh, the capital of Assyria, after the Tigris River flooded and washed away part of the earthen walls that protected it. In 605 BC, Nebuchadnezzar of Babylon subdued Jerusalem and appointed Jehoiakim a vassal king. Nebuchadnezzar took some of the noble class of Jews, including Daniel, Shadrack, Meshack, and Abed-nego back to Babylon. In 586 BC, when then Babylon's vassal king Zedekiah tried to rebel against Nebuchadnezzar, Nebuchadnezzar brought his army back and sacked Jerusalem and destroyed the temple and exiled thousands of Jews to Babylon.

When the Judeans continued to resist Babylonian capture, Jeremiah knew that God was using Babylon as a tool to punish them and that resistance would mean death. He told them, "Go to Babylon and live." God does not tell anyone to die for their faith. God told (through Jeremiah) the Jews to go to Babylon and establish a life there. From this, we get one of the most wonderful promises of God in the Bible: *"For I know the plans that I have for you,' declares the Lord, 'plans for welfare and not for calamity, to give you a future and a hope. Then you will call upon Me and come and pray to Me, and I will listen to you. And you will seek Me and find Me, when you search for Me with all your heart"* (Jeremiah 29:11–13).

Jeremiah continued to minister to Judah after the exile until about 580 BC.

The Lamentations of Jeremiah

The Lamentations of Jeremiah is the poetry Jeremiah wrote in his grief over the loss of the Jews' beloved city, Jerusalem, and the historic temple built over 350 years before. Jeremiah, like Jesus, was known as the weeping prophet. In John 11:35, Jesus wept over the news of Lazarus's death. Jesus, as he approached the day of his crucifixion, wept for Jerusalem, knowing that in a few years, the temple would be destroyed by the Romans. Jesus, the greatest prophet and Son of God, went to Jerusalem to turn people's hearts and minds back to God, but He said, *"But you were unwilling"* (Matthew 23:37).

Jeremiah's faith was great and unperturbed. He understood that God was imposing judgment on His people, and he knew that God would restore them in the future. Love oftentimes requires discipline, and this was God's discipline out of love. Jeremiah said, *"The Lord's lovingkindnesses indeed never cease, for His compassions never fail. They are new every morning; great is thy faithfulness"* (Lamentations 3:22–23).

Ezekiel

Ezekiel was a priest and prophet who was carried off to Babylon in 597 BC, where he joined Daniel. Daniel was taken to Babylon about eight years earlier, when Nebuchadnezzar first subdued Jerusalem. Egypt invaded Judah and appointed vassal kings in 609 BC. Backing up a bit, in 609 BC, Josiah, the last of the good kings of Judah, unadvisedly entered the battlefield against Pharaoh Neco of Egypt and was killed by Neco. Neco placed Jehoiakim and then Jehoiachin as vassal kings of Judah. In 597 BC, Nebuchadnezzar pushed out the Egyptians and installed Zedekiah as his vassal king. In 586 BC, Zedekiah conspired with Egypt to overthrow Babylon's yoke, and when Nebuchadnezzar learned of it, he went to Jerusalem and sacked it and destroyed the temple. He then took tens of thousands of Jews to Babylon in fulfillment of previous prophesies.

During the ten years after Ezekiel was taken to Babylon, Jeremiah remained in Jerusalem, and they both continued to condemn their brethren for their unfaithfulness and sins. Ezekiel, in chapters 4 through 24, prophesied the judgment against Judah to the exiles in Babylon at the same time that Jeremiah was doing the same in Jerusalem to the soon-to-be-exiled Jews.

While there are several apparent allusions to Jesus in Ezekiel, they are not entirely clear. The most obvious allusion occurs in Ezekiel 34:22–24 when Ezekiel prophesies, "*I will set over them one shepherd, my servant David, and he will feed them; he will feed them himself and be their shepherd.*" This is referring to the future Messiah, Jesus, of the house of David, who will be the shepherd over God's people. Ezekiel's message included hope for the future, emphasizing the glorious sovereignty of God.

Daniel

Daniel was a member of the royal family of Judah, who was taken to Babylon as a captive of

Nebuchadnezzar when he first subdued Jerusalem in about 605 BC. He was an exceptionally intelligent young man of about seventeen and was given exceptional privileges in the king's court. The story of Daniel spans the entire seventy years of Judah's exile. Daniel was in King Belshazzar's court when Babylon was defeated by the Persians under Cyrus the Great in 539 BC. Cyrus then decreed that a temple to the great God would be built in Jerusalem. Cyrus encouraged all Jews to go to Jerusalem to help build the temple. There is no record that Daniel ever returned to Judah.

Daniel had a particular God-given gift of understanding of dreams and visions. When the king had one really strange dream, he demanded that his wise men and magicians tell him what he had dreamed and what was its meaning. Of course, no one can tell what another person dreamed, but God gave to Daniel that ability. When Daniel correctly told Nebuchadnezzar what he had dreamed and the interpretation of that dream, the king promoted him to ruler over the local province and prefect over the wise men of Babylon. Daniel also had the king appoint his three friends—Shadrack, Meshack, and Abed-nego—as administrators of the province.

In Daniel is the account of his three friends refusing to worship the statue of the king and being thrown into a fiery furnace as punishment for their rebellion. God miraculously delivered Shadrack, Meshack, and

Abed-nego from the fire. Here we see the foreshadow-ing of a savior whom God provided to save us from the fires of hell because of our disobedience to a righteous and holy God. Later when Daniel refused to obey a foolish decree of the king put forth by jealous leaders who wanted to see Daniel's demise, Daniel was thrown into a den of lions. God spared Daniel. The king real-ized what had transpired, and he had the conspirators thrown into the lion's den where they were quickly overcome and killed.

Other key events of Daniel are the visions he had which prophesied events that would occur in the future. He prophesied the defeat of the Persian Empire by the Greeks, which transpired under Alexander the Great less than three hundred years later. He prophesied the rise of the Roman Empire, and finally, the coming of the Messiah to Jerusalem on a specific date which proved true. When Jesus entered Jerusalem at age thirty-three, the date coincided exactly with Daniel's prophecy.

The Minor Prophets

Hosea to Malachi

The twelve books of the minor prophets are called minor because they are short as compared with the length of the major prophets. The messages of all seventeen prophets are equally important—that is that the Israelite people turn back to God.

Hosea

The name Hosea means salvation and comes from the same Hebrew root word giving us the name Jesus. Jesus means "Yahweh is salvation." Hosea's message was one of salvation: turn back to God and receive salvation. Hosea ministered to the northern kingdom from mid-eighth century until after Assyria conquered them in 722 BC. So we see that Hosea was a contemporary of Isaiah and Micah, who ministered to the southern kingdom of Judah.

I alluded earlier to riches being a possible cause of Israel's turning away from God. Hosea 10:1–2 says, *"Israel is a luxuriant vine; He produces fruit for himself, The more his fruit, the more altars he made; the richer his land, the better he made the sacred pillars."* Because Israel prostituted herself for the sake of riches, God told Hosea to marry a prostitute, to demonstrate to Israel the reality of their sin. After marrying Gomer, a prostitute, and having three children, Gomer still goes after and has other lovers, further demonstrating Israel's unfaithfulness to God. Hosea finds her and has to pay money to redeem her, demonstrating God's willingness to take Israel back from its idolatrous ways.

Joel

This book may be the most difficult to understand as it gives no good clues to its time. The plague of locusts Joel writes about may be a prophecy of a large army invasion or a real natural calamity. If the former, then we might think it was prior to Babylon's invasion of Judah and the exiling of Jews to Babylon. His message to the Jews is that they repent and turn back to God. In the book of Acts, Peter said that the events concerning the Messiah's death had been foretold by Joel.

Amos

A contemporary of Hosea in Israel, Amos was from Judah, but his message was to the northern kingdom. Amos ministered for a period of about eight years, around 760–753 BC during the time under Jeroboam II. This was a prosperous age, with Israel controlling the trade routes which ran through it. Jeroboam was an evil king and gave no heed to the personal conduct of his people. Israel had backslidden, and God told Amos to go to Jeroboam and give him the message that Israel was heading toward destruction unless they reversed course. Being from Judah, Amos's message was not well-received.

Obadiah

The time of Obadiah cannot be determined with a great degree of certainty. In verse 18, Obadiah speaks of the house of Jacob, which is Judah and the house of Joseph which is Israel, also known at times as Ephraim, who was the son of Joseph. It appears the time was before either of the northern or southern kingdoms were defeated and exiled. Obadiah's vision concerned the judgment on Edom, who had been a thorn in the Israelite's side since the Edomites denied passage to the Israelites as they neared the Promised Land from their journey from Egypt's captivity. During the time of Elisha, the prophet in Israel, King Hazael of Aram warred against King Jehoram of Judah, and the Edomites who had been under the sovereignty of Judah saw fit to rebel during this time of turmoil. Obadiah felt that Edom should have united with Judah against Israel, and when she gloated over the defeat of Jehoram, Obadiah declared that Edom would be destroyed.

My opinion is that this book of prophecy does not belong in the Bible at all because it does not address the disobedience of Judah toward God and the necessity to call Judah to task for their disobedience. It is not referenced in the New Testament at all. It is just a case of Obadiah, an unknown person, having written a diatribe against a longtime enemy of Judah, who took advantage of an opportunity to gain their freedom from Judah. The decreed punishment of Edom was not brought about by Judah but by Babylon.

The allusions to Christ in Obadiah can be seen in verse 15, *"For the day of the Lord draws near on all the nations."* Obadiah sees the coming of a Messiah who will triumph over all and give Judah its rightful place.

Jonah

This short book has no genealogical connection to Jesus and does not address any disobedience of God by the Jewish people. Instead, it is God reaching out to a non-Jewish people to invite them to turn to Him and away from their wickedness. In Jonah, God demonstrates his love to all humanity by sending Jonah to Nineveh to preach repentance to a large city who were displaying conduct that was repulsive to God.

When the Lord told Jonah to go to Nineveh and preach to them, Jonah rebelled and tried to hide from God by travelling to the very edge of civilization. Jonah boarded a ship headed for Tarsus in Spain. Perhaps as a dedicated Hebrew, Jonah should have been aware of the Psalm by David, which says, in essence, "Wherever I go, O God, you are there" (Psalms 139:7–8). Here is a lesson for us as well: We cannot hide from God. God caused a storm in the Mediterranean Sea, in which the ship was floundering. The crew cast lots to see who on board was responsible for this catastrophe, and the lot fell on Jonah. They cast him overboard to save themselves. God sent a great fish or sea monster to swallow Jonah and preserve him. After the fish spit Jonah up on shore, Jonah obeyed and went to Nineveh to preach repentance to them. The Ninevites heard him and repented. Nineveh was the capital of Assyria, which later would defeat Israel (the northern kingdom) and totally displace the Jews from Israel to places throughout the Assyrian Empire.

Jesus spoke of Jonah when he replied to the Pharisees who asked Jesus for a sign to prove that He was the Messiah. Jesus said, *"As Jonah was in the belly of the sea monster for three days and three nights, the Son of Man shall be in the heart of the earth."* The Pharisees would not understand what Jesus was saying until Jesus was crucified and arose from the dead after three days. So Jonah was a type of Christ in that his being in the belly of the sea monster signified the future death, burial, and resurrection of Jesus.

Micah

This is an awesome book of prophecy written by Micah and tells of God's message to both Judah and Israel to repent of their evil ways. One of the great sins of Judah and Israel was the mistreatment of the poor, widows, and orphans of their own people, something God explicitly forbade in the law. Micah writes of a litany of sins common among the people. God called Micah to speak out against these sins and also revealed to Micah that Babylon, which was over a hundred years away from becoming its own independent country, would, in future times, overcome Judah and carry her off in exile (Micah 4:10).

In Micah 5:2, we see the clearest prophecy in the Old Testament of the birth of a savior in the town of Bethlehem, "*One who existed from eternity to come forth and rule over Israel.*"

In Micah 6:8, he provides the antidote for the malignancy of sin: "*He has told you, O man, what is good; and what does the Lord require of you but to do justice, to love kindness, and to walk humbly with your God?*" There is no more important thing in this book I want you to understand than what this verse says. It is basically a rewording of the greatest commandments given by God as repeated by Jesus: "You shall love the Lord thy God with all your heart and love your neighbor as yourself."

Nahum

Nahum was from Elkosh, a place that has never been identified as to location. Three possible locations in Israel or Judah and one north of Nineveh have been suggested, with scholars accepting a location in southern Judah as the most likely. However, a tomb of

Nahum has been sighted in the city north of Nineveh, which is today known as Alqosh, Iraq. I believe Nahum was from the location north of Nineveh for that reason and the following:

In 722 BC, Assyria, whose capital was Nineveh, conquered Israel and displaced the ten tribes to the kingdom of Assyria and brought inhabitants of Assyria to Israel to live. That put a large population of Jews in locations all over Assyria. Nahum was most likely one of those displaced Jews from Israel living in Elkosh.

A hundred years earlier, Jonah had gone to Nineveh from Israel to preach repentance to the Ninevites. When Nineveh returned to its old sinful ways, God used Nahum to declare that Nineveh, a virtually impossible city to overthrow because of its fortress construction, would be destroyed by an overflowing flood. Nineveh, situated by the Tigris River, was inside a fortress constructed of dirt one hundred feet tall and wide enough to allow three chariots to travel abreast. It was considered impregnable. However, in 612 BC, the Tigris River overflowed and washed away one of the dirt walls, and the army of Babylon went through the gap, defeated Assyria, and totally destroyed the city. Whereas Assyria had been attacking the fortified cities of Judah; now Babylon became the empire most dangerous to Judah.

There are no genealogical connections to Jesus in the book of Nahum. Chapter 1 verses 2–8 give the characteristics of the Lord being an avenging God and slow to anger. In that vein, we can insert Jesus as co-God, because in John 1:1, we read, *"In the beginning was the Word, and the Word was with God, and the Word was God. He [Jesus] was in the beginning with God."*

Zephaniah

A prophet during the reign of Josiah, Zephaniah's message of reform was apparently too little, too late. Zephaniah's message was the same as the prophets who came before him into the courts of the king of Judah: *"repent and turn back to God from your idolatrous ways or destruction awaits you."* Joash was only eight years old when he took the throne of Judah, and it was some eight years later that he began reforms that would bring the worship of Yahweh back to Judah. Joash became king after fifty-five years of rule by the evilest of all the kings of Judah, Manasseh and Amon, so there was an ingrained culture of idol worship and immorality that would take years to overcome.

The die had been cast, so to speak. Josiah reigned thirty-one years, but his reforms came too slowly. Josiah was killed by Neco, the king of Egypt, in 609 BC, who placed his own vassal king on the throne of Judah. Just four years later, Babylon would subdue Jerusalem and put its vassal king on Judah's throne, setting the stage for the total destruction of Judah in 586 BC, when

Zedekiah, Babylon's vassal king of Judah, conspired with Egypt to overthrow Babylon's yoke.

There is no specific mention of Jesus or Messiah in Zephaniah, but there is a vague allusion to a Messiah. The promise of restoration of Judah in chapter 3 includes a future king in their midst to be a victor over disaster and enemies of God.

Haggai

In 539 BC, the Persians under Cyrus the Great overthrew Babylon and decreed that a temple would be built for the great God in Jerusalem. All Jews who desired could go to Jerusalem to help in the effort. As had been prophesied, after seventy years of captivity, the Jews were now free to return to their homeland. Two priests and prophets of Judah, Haggai and Zachariah, returned to Judah with the first remnant under the leadership of Zerubbabel and Joshua, the high priest. These two were instrumental in getting the temple rebuild completed after work lagged, then stopped because of opposition by neighboring Samaria. Also, the fact that they had not built houses to live in for themselves, which they decided do before completing the temple, delayed it.

The Jews returned to a desolate country, where crop failure, hard work, and opposition faced them in their endeavors to rebuild Jerusalem and the temple.

After only two years, work on the temple stopped. It was restarted fourteen years later, when Haggai and Zechariah used their positions as priests to cajole and encourage the work to be done. Haggai used some shaming of the remnant (those few Jews who returned to Judah) to get them restarted on building the temple. He told them that the ground was withholding its produce from them because they were taking care of their own personal needs before the need of finishing the temple.

Haggai prophesies in his zeal to get the temple built that all nations will contribute to the glory of the temple, and that its glory will exceed that of the previous temple. Herod the Great, in the two decades before the birth of Christ, enlarged and enriched the temple, which might be considered as preparation for the Messiah's arrival. Zerubbabel, a direct ancestor of Jesus, is prophesied (declared by God) to become like a signet ring because God chose him to be a type of Messiah, like Moses, in his leadership role, leading the remnant back to the Promised Land and rebuilding the temple, the tabernacle of God.

Zachariah

As in Haggai, the remnant of Jews need encouragement to restart and complete the building of the temple. Zechariah reminded the remnant of the pre-exilic words of the prophets, *"Return to me that I may return to you."* Their failure to do that led to their exile.

Zechariah has a vision in which he sees Joshua the High Priest in filthy clothes standing before the Lord with Satan present, accusing Joshua. The high priest was to be clothed in richly made clothing fitting for the office. Zechariah realizes that the remnant must throw off their filthy rags and clothe themselves in righteousness by speaking the truth to one another—judging with truth and judgment for peace in their gates. Joshua, whose name is a form of the name Jesus, meaning salvation, was to lead this flock in righteous living. God had given the Jews a new start and the promise of a glorious future—a future where people of all nations would come to seek the lord of hosts in Jerusalem. This was Zechariah's vision of the Messiah, who would return to Jerusalem and be the God of all nations.

Malachi

This is the last prophetic utterance to the Jews for four hundred years until John the Baptist came, the voice of one crying in the wilderness, *"Make ready the way of the Lord."* Malachi is unknown as to his heritage or parents. Malachi is a devout Jew and fervent in his devotion to God, and he sees failure in the priests to adequately serve the people. Some eighty years after, the temple is rebuilt in Jerusalem, the people are in a rut of discontent in their worship, just going through the motions, so to speak. God sent Malachi to call out the priests as well as the people for their lukewarm attitude, their hypocrisy in worshipping God.

Malachi says they (the people) have resorted to offering defective and sick animals for sacrifice, neglecting to bring their tithes and offerings to the temple and neglecting the wives of their youth and going after foreign wives. God says to them to bring the whole tithe into the storehouse *and "Test me now and see if I will not open for you the windows of heaven and pour out for you a blessing until it overflows"* (Malachi 3:10).

In chapter 3:1, Malachi prophesies that God *"will send a messenger who will clear the way before Me."* This speaks of John the Baptist, who will precede and announce the arrival of the greatest prophet of all, Jesus Christ, after a period of silence of four hundred years.

PART 2

THE NEW TESTAMENT

I have written this summary of the New Testament because it is my purpose to help you make sense of the whole Bible. My desire is that people read the whole Bible through cover to cover. I hope these book summaries encourage you to do that.

CHAPTER 13

THE GOSPELS

The New Testament is the good news of Jesus Christ, particularly, the first four books which are called the gospels, which means good news. The gospels—Matthew, Mark, Luke, and John—each contain most of the same history of Jesus, each with some differences from the others. In the gospels, we learn about the birth of Jesus to which the Old Testament in its entirety points. In the Old Testament, He was the coming Messiah. In the New Testament, He is the Messiah who has come. Jesus is the Messiah, not just a prophet. He is the Son of God, incarnate, meaning He was here in human fleshly form.

Matthew

Let's start with the book of Matthew. It begins with the ancestry of Jesus from Adam to Mary and Joseph and finally to Jesus. While the Old Testament prophets foretold of the coming of the Messiah, Matthew heralds the arrival of Jesus, born in Bethlehem, which birthplace was also foretold by the prophets.

Matthew was a tax collector in the Roman government in Capernaum and was disliked by his fellow countrymen. He came to know Jesus when he heard Jesus talking, most likely when Jesus gave what is called the Sermon on the Mount near Capernaum where Matthew was from. The Sermon on the Mount are probably the most famous words spoken by Jesus, particularly the Beatitudes found in Matthew chapter 5. Matthew became a disciple of Jesus there and was later named an apostle. It is interesting that Jesus would allow a tax collector as an apostle. People thought of tax collectors as cheats, collecting more than they were supposed to. Jesus had thousands of disciples, which actually means followers, but Jesus named only twelve as apostles, those disciples who were closest to Him. These twelve apostles were found near Jesus most of the time. Why did Jesus select a tax collector as an apostle? Matthew, if he was a cheater, now followed Christ's teaching, and Jesus found him to be worthy as a follower.

In chapter 3 of Matthew, John the Baptist is introduced as one who came preaching in the wilderness, saying, *"Repent for the kingdom of heaven is at hand."* John the Baptist was referred to and foretold in Malachi in the Old Testament. Isaiah 40:3 says, *"The voice of one crying in the wilderness, make ready the way of the Lord."* People from Jerusalem would come out to the Jordan River where John the Baptist preached to and baptized them. When some Pharisees came for baptism, he called them a brood of vipers and admonished them to bring forth fruit in keeping with repentance. He also said to those who came to him, *"I baptize you with water for repentance, but He who is coming after me is mightier than I, and I am not fit to remove His sandals; He will baptize you with the Holy Spirit and fire"* (John 3:11). While John was teaching and baptizing at the Jordan River, Jesus came to him to be baptized. John recognized Jesus for who He was and felt unworthy to baptize Jesus. He told Jesus that he wanted to be baptized by Jesus, evidently wanting to be baptized with the Holy Spirit.

After Jesus was baptized by John, He was led by the Spirit into the wilderness to be tempted by the devil. Satan tempted Jesus to perform supernatural things and promised Jesus He would be sovereign over the kingdoms of the earth if He would bow down and worship him. Jesus spoke directly to Satan with force from the scriptures, saying, *"You shall not put the Lord your God to the test"* (Matthew 7:7) and *"You shall worship the Lord your God and serve Him only"* (Matthew 7:10).

When John the Baptist spoke to the Pharisees so critically, they were incensed; and having the power to do so, they had the magistrates of that area place him under arrest, mostly for what they called heresy against the laws of God. Later in chapter 14, Matthew recounts the beheading of John the Baptist by King Herod, when Herod put his foot in his mouth by promising the beautiful Salome, whose dancing pleased him so greatly that he would give her anything she wanted. The girl's mother told her to ask for John the Baptist's head on a platter. This was because John had been publicly critical of Herod for taking his brother's wife. Herod could not go back on his oath, and he, sadly, had to carry through with his promise.

It is in the book of Matthew that we find the discourse between Jesus and Simon Peter, where Jesus asked Peter, *"Who do people say that I am?"* Peter answered. *"You are the Christ, the Son of the Living God."* Jesus replied, *"Blessed are you Simon Bar Jonah, because flesh and blood did not reveal this to you, but My Father who is in heaven. I say to you that you are Peter, and upon this rock I will build My church, and the gates of Hades shall not overpower it. I will give you the keys of the kingdom of heaven and whatsoever you shall bind on earth shall be bound in heaven and whatever you shall loose on earth shall be loosed in heaven"* (Matthew 16:13–19). The "keys" to the kingdom of heaven is the authority Jesus gave to the apostles to open the doors of heaven by carrying on the gospel of Jesus after He had fulfilled His mission on earth and ascended into heaven. The name

Peter was derived from the Greek word *petros*, which means "rock."

What a heavy burden to put on Peter. But it was not on Peter only, but to all the apostles to whom he was talking. When Jesus said, *"Upon this rock I will build My church…,"* he was saying that Peter's faith was the foundation stone upon which the church would carry on. Jesus saw Peter as the most solid of the believing disciples and gave him the keys to the kingdom of heaven. That is why Peter is considered the first pope of the Catholic Church.

In chapter 12, there occurs a critical event when the Pharisees, the acting leaders of the Jewish nation, formally rejected Jesus as the Messiah, saying that His power was derived from Satan rather than from God. Pharisees were well-founded in scripture; all Pharisees memorized the Pentateuch as part of their training. So they were the experts on the law. But they were blinded by the law and refused to see who was in front of them. They were only interested in the letter of the law and not the intent—that is, that we love Him and treat other people with love and respect.

From that point on, Jesus taught lessons by what are known as parables, which some have simply defined as earthly stories with a heavenly meaning. Actually, the Pharisees demanded a sign from Him, but instead of performing miracles, he told these stories, or parables, which dealt with the kingdom of God. Some parables even parodied the Pharisees, which only added to their dislike and ire for him.

Even though Jesus performed miracles, He did not do them on demand. Jesus performed miracles when there was a specific need, such as making a blind person to see or making a crippled person walk. He usually did this out of compassion, and when He specifically asked a person what he or she needed. Sometimes someone would recognize Him as the Son of God and ask to be healed. In each case, Jesus said that it was their faith that healed them.

Jesus taught his disciples to pray in the form we know as the Lord's Prayer. He also taught about the giving of alms, both to the church, and to help people in need. He taught that our focus should not be on attaining to wealth, which we can become a slave to, but giving attention to loving and serving God. He said, "*Where your treasure it, there your heart will be also. No man can serve two masters, for either he will hate the one and love the other, or he will hold to one and despise the other. You cannot serve God and mammon*" (Matthew 6:24). Jesus talked more about money than anything, except the kingdom of God. He talked about money and treasure because he knows it affects our hearts, either for joy or for grief.

But perhaps most important of his teachings was what we refer to as the Golden Rule: "The way you want people to treat you, that is the way you should treat them." We know it best as *"Do unto others as you would have them do unto you"* (Matthew 7:12).

Mark

In the book of Mark, we find many parables and miracles, some of which are unique to Mark's writings. In Mark, we are again introduced to John the Baptist and his baptism of Jesus. Mark mentions that following Jesus's baptism, Jesus went into the wilderness for forty days, where He was tempted by Satan, but he gives no details. The details of Jesus's wilderness experience with Satan are spelled out in the books of Matthew and Luke. In Mark, there are many accounts of Jesus's miracles of healing and feeding thousands of people who had come to hear Him teach.

As mentioned earlier, Jesus spoke a lot about money and wealth. In Mark 10:23, Jesus says, "How hard it will be for those who are wealthy to enter the kingdom of God." He said, *"It is easier for a camel to go through the eye of a needle than for a rich man to enter the kingdom of God."* Obviously, a camel cannot be put through the eye of a sewing needle, but here, he is talking about the small opening in the wall of a city where people could enter after the cities gates were closed. The wall opening is in the shape of a needle and is actually called a needle and is large enough for a person to walk through. A camel could enter by crawling on its knees with much difficulty. So it is possible for a wealthy person to enter the kingdom of God if he or she is using those riches to care for the widows, orphans, and poor people. It is when our wealth becomes our only focus and takes our eyes off God that it becomes a bar to the kingdom.

The Parable of the Sower of Seed in chapter 4 is the second of ten parables in Mark, and in it, Jesus taught that the gospel is like seeds broadcast by a sower. Like seeds that fall on different types of soil and are eaten by the birds, on rocky ground where it springs up quickly but has to water of nutrients, in thorny patches where the plant is choked out and yields no crop, and some fall on good soil and grow and yield a good crop, so is the gospel. As seeds that fall on the road where birds eat it, the gospel falls on deaf ears blocked by Satan. As the seed on the rocky ground springs up quickly but withers, the gospel is initially accepted but does not sink in deeply, and when hard times come, people give up. As the seed that falls among the thorns, the gospel is choked out by the cares of the world. As seeds that fall on good soil, people accept the gospel and apply it to their lives and even produce more fruit by sharing the gospel with others. If Jesus were here today, he would probably end this discussion by uttering, "I'm just saying."

The key takeaway for the book of Mark is that Jesus was a servant who constantly ministered to people in need. The Gospel of Mark ends with the betrayal of Jesus by Judas, one of his twelve apostles, and being taken into custody and taken to trial by Pontius Pilate, who was the Roman Prefect for Jerusalem, and finally with Jesus's being crucified on a cross. He describes Jesus's burial, His resurrection, and His appearance before a number of people before He was taken up into heaven.

Luke

The gospel according to Luke was written by Luke, who also wrote the book of Acts, formally named "The Acts of the Apostles." Later, Paul, in Colossians 4:14, called Luke the beloved physician. So Luke was actually a doctor, making him capable of traveling with Paul and, as a historian, establishing the reality of who Jesus was. Luke possibly lived during a portion of the time that Jesus was on earth because he accompanied the Apostle Paul on his journeys and learned most of the things that he wrote about Jesus from Paul. We can assume that Paul also lived during the time of Jesus on earth because he was a contemporary of Peter. There is no record of any encounter between Paul and Jesus, except after Jesus's death, when Jesus appeared to Paul, then called Saul, on the road to Damascus, when Saul was looking for Christians to bring before the Sanhedrin for persecution. That account is in the book of Acts.

Like Matthew, Luke also recounts the ancestry of Jesus, but his ancestry works backward from Joseph and Mary to Adam and is actually the ancestry through Mary, not Joseph. The book of Luke contains the story of the conception of Mary by the Holy Spirit and the subsequent birth of Jesus in Bethlehem in a stable, where livestock were kept. It is the passage of the Bible most often read by Christians when celebrating Christmas each year. Luke also covers the ministry of John the Baptist and the temptation of Christ by the devil in the wilderness after his baptism by John the Baptist.

The book of Luke is replete with parables and instances of healing of the sick and infirmed. In chapter 22, we read where the chief priests and scribes paid Judas to betray Jesus, and Jesus calls him out for his impending betrayal during His final meal on earth, which we know as The Last Supper. It was during this meal that Jesus told Peter that before the cock would crow that day, Peter would deny Him three times that day. Peter asserted that would never happen. This was two days before the celebration of the Passover, the day that Jesus died. This is incredible. The Passover in Egypt was a foreshadowing of Jesus's death on the cross, sacrificing his blood for the payment of our debt of sin. Jesus's death on the very day of Passover was no coincidence.

Luke then tells of Judas's acceptance of money from the chief priests to betray Jesus. Judas led the chief priests to the garden of Gethsemane while Jesus was there praying that God, His Father, would spare Him from the death He was about to suffer. However, Jesus said, *"Not My will, but Thine be done"* (Luke 22:42). Though we may not be called to give our life for a cause, there may occur many difficult decisions that we must make; and when we pray to God for his guidance, our prayer should be, "Not my will, but thine be done."

After Jesus's arrest, Peter came near to the place where Jesus was taken to keep an eye on Him. When asked by a girl who was there if he, Peter, wasn't one of the followers of Jesus, Peter denied it, even to the point of cursing, saying, "Heck no! I do not know him." His language was probably a bit saltier than that. After his third vehement denial, Peter heard a cock crow and remembered what the Lord had said, and immediately, Peter went out and wept bitterly. Luke then ends his writing in Luke with the trial of Christ by Pontius Pilate, the crucifixion, burial, and the resurrection of Christ.

Luke's purpose in writing the book of Luke was to reveal the results of his extensive research on exactly who Jesus was. Luke was really a historian listing the events of Jesus's life on earth from his birth to his crucifixion and resurrection. Luke emphasized Jesus's humanity in

Jesus's showing love and compassion to the unlovable and to the sick.

John

The Gospel of John was written by the apostle John, one of the twelve Jesus named back in the book of Matthew. After Jesus ascended into heaven, following His crucifixion, John became one of the pillars of the church. John refers to himself as the disciple whom Jesus loved. It is John who is portrayed in Leonardo da Vinci's painting, *The Last Supper*, leaning back against Jesus's breast.

Chapter 1 verses 1–4 reads, *"In the beginning was the Word, and the Word was with God, and the Word was God. He was in the beginning with God. All things came into being by Him, and apart from Him nothing came into being that has come into being. In Him was life, and the life was the light of men."*

This passage is talking about Jesus. In the beginning, He was with God. Being with God suggests a separate personality and now Jesus is introduced on earth as a baby, in the flesh, born of a virgin. I do not doubt the virgin birth, whether it is possible or not. How difficult would it be for God, who created all things, to create a child in a virgin girl?

Why did God choose to send someone in the form of a human? Why not an angel or some kind of spiritual being? Because we, as humans, cannot relate to angels or spiritual beings. Angels and spiritual beings are not like us. We would have no one to show us in earthly human means how to live a godly life. Jesus came to demonstrate how life is to be lived, not as an earthly king, but as one of us. We can relate to Him. He came not only to demonstrate to us how to live; He came as the Son of God to demonstrate perfection and as the Son of God to receive the penalty of our sins for us.

Romans 3:23 says, *"For all have sinned and come short of the glory of God."* Romans 6:23 says, *"For the wages of sin is death, but the gift of God is eternal life in Christ Jesus our Lord."* Solomon said in his prayer for understanding, "For there is no one who is perfect." We sin. Is that the end? No. God sent Jesus Christ for the very purpose of dying on the cross to pay our penalty for sin. Christ, who knew no sin, became sin for us that we may become the righteousness of God in Him (2 Corinthians 5:21).

The book of John, more than any other New Testament book, is about God's love for us and contains what may be the most well-known verse in the Bible, John 3:16. *"For God so loved the world that He gave His only begotten Son, that whosoever believeth on him shall not perish but have everlasting life."*

John begins his gospel by asserting the deity of Christ. *"In the beginning was the Word, and the Word was with God, and the Word was God"* (John 1:1). John then tells of John the Baptist, who was a forerunner of Christ and his baptism of Jesus. The record of Jesus's first miracle is told, that of Jesus changing water into wine at the wedding in Cana. John relates much of the life of Jesus and His encounters with many diverse people, how He healed many of them, and the feeding of thousands of people who had come to hear Him speak, with only five loaves of bread and two fish.

One of the most instructive encounters of Jesus was with a woman who was caught in the very act of adultery. The Pharisees brought this woman to Him, hoping to catch Jesus off guard and accuse Him to the Sanhedrin. The Pharisees said to him, "*Teacher, this woman has been caught in adultery, in the very act. In the Law Moses commanded us to stone such women; what then do You say?*" Jesus said to them, "*Let he who is without sin be the first to cast a stone.*" The Pharisees and all the onlookers hung their heads, and one by one began to leave. Jesus then said to the woman, "*Woman, where are your accusers? Did no one condemn you?*" The woman replied, "*No one, Lord.*" Jesus said, "*Neither do I condemn you; go your way. From now on sin no more*" (John 8:1-8) He probably said something like, "Go and try not to sin" since perfection was only attained by Jesus Himself.

What a lesson for us. Jesus does not judge; He left that job to God. Jesus did not condemn. What are your thoughts about certain sins? Is any sin greater or less than another? Sin is sin. What about abortion and homosexuality? Abortion is not addressed in the Bible. Homosexuality is not addressed directly in the New Testament.

Homosexuality has existed for thousands of years, yet we have no record of Jesus addressing it. Leviticus speaks only of males lying with another male, it does not address females. When people ask me about whether homosexuality is a sin, I respond I am not sure, but God did not put me on this earth to judge people. All humans have a need for human intimacy, closeness, and trust. Everyone has to make up their own minds about attaining this intimacy and be prepared to appear before God to answer for all their actions, both good and bad.

In Luke 18:11–13, we find this account: *"A Pharisee stood in front of others to pray. He thanked God that he was better than other people. He said that he fasted two times each week and paid his tithing. A tax gatherer stood by himself, bowed his head, and prayed, 'God be merciful to me a sinner."* Jesus said that this man went down to his house justified, rather than the other—for everyone who exalts himself shall be humbled, but he who humbles himself shall be exalted. That is what we all are, sinners. We have no right to stand in judgment of anyone, regardless of his or her sin. Let us be honest with God and confess our own sins. We must be humble in all things.

Truly enlightening of John's gospel is his portrayal of Jesus's humanity. He writes of Jesus's weariness, thirst, grief, anguish, and death. We can relate. Most important of all in John's gospel is the individual's response to Jesus. Those who believe and put their faith in Jesus have life; those who do not are condemned by God.

CHAPTER 14

ACTS

The formal name of this book is the *Acts of the Apostles*. The apostles were those selected by Jesus as his closest adherents and to whom were entrusted the keys to the kingdom of heaven. This book tells about the apostles' actions after Jesus was resurrected as the formal title indicates. Acts was written by Luke who accompanied the apostle Paul on his journeys to establish churches in Asia Minor and is referred to by Paul as the beloved physician. Paul considered himself an apostle, even though he had not encountered Jesus while Jesus walked on the earth. After he was accosted by Jesus on the road to Damascus when he was searching out Christians for persecution and even death, he became *"a chosen instrument of Mine, to bear My name before the Gentiles and kings and the sons of Israel…"* (Jesus speaking through Ananias in Acts 9:15).

Acts begins with Jesus having reappeared to the apostles and about five hundred people after His resurrection, telling them that He would baptize them not many days hence, not with water but with the Holy Spirit. He said, *"You shall have power when the Holy Spirit comes upon you, and you shall be My witnesses both in Jerusalem, and in all Judea and Samaria, and even to the remotest part of the earth"* (Acts 1:8). After He said this, He was taken up into heaven.

Shortly thereafter, on the day of Pentecost, Peter delivered a lengthy discourse, explaining that all that had happened concerning the Messiah was foretold by the prophets Joel and David. Peter was speaking to a diverse group of Jews who were not followers of Jesus and very pointedly blamed them for nailing to the cross the Son of God. He said, *"Therefore, let all the house of Israel know for certain that God has made Him both Lord and Christ—this Jesus whom you crucified."* When they heard this, they were pierced to the heart and said to Peter, *"Brethren, what shall we do?"* Peter said to them, *"Repent and let each of you be baptized in the name of Jesus Christ for the forgiveness of your sins, and you shall receive the gift of the Holy Spirit"* (Acts 2:36–38). The gift of the Holy Spirit does not mean that you will suddenly start speaking in tongues or understanding a language that is not your own as is what happened on the day of Pentecost. On that day, when Jesus gave the Holy Spirit to the apostles and Jews gathered together, the group gathered there were of diverse cultures and languages, and each man heard the Holy Spirit speaking in his own language. The gift of the Holy Spirit is grace. We receive the grace of God when we repent. As Jesus said in John, *"I will send a comforter to you"* (John 14:16). The Holy Spirit is Jesus with us in spirit form.

In Ephesians 2:8–9, Paul says, *"For by grace you have been saved through faith, and that not of yourselves, it is the gift of God; not as a result of works that you do, so that no one can boast."*

Now the Sanhedrin, a group of ruling Pharisees, did not like what Peter was preaching, which is no surprise since they crucified Jesus for much the same reason. They told Peter and John to stop their preaching about Jesus. But Peter, being the bold, impetuous fellow he was, along with John, said, *"Whether it is right in the sight of God to give heed to you rather than to God, you be the judge; for we cannot stop speaking what we have seen and heard"* (Acts 4:19).

When Peter and John were brought before the council to be questioned by the high priest, they basically said the same thing, that they must obey God rather than man. They said, *"You put to death on the cross Jesus whom God sent us. He is the one whom God exalted to His right hand as a Prince and a Savior, to grant repentance to Israel and forgiveness of sins. And we are witnesses of these things, and so is the Holy Spirit, whom God has given to those who obey Him"* (Acts 5:30–32).

Wow! Did this anger the priests or what? The priests were intending to slay Peter and John as they had Jesus, but a certain Pharisee by the name of Gamaliel stood up in the council and sent Peter and John outside so he could address the council. He told them of various groups with certain disturbing agendas who, after some time, as their cause was no longer popular, went away. Gamaliel said, *"In the present case, I say stay away from these men and let them alone, for if this plan or action should be of men, it shall be overthrown, but if it is of God, you will not be able to overthrow them, or else you may even be found fighting against God"* (Acts 5:38–39). So they took his advice and admonished Peter and John to no longer speak in the name of Jesus and then released them. Later, we learn that Paul studied to be a Pharisee at the feet of Gamaliel.

It was about this time that the apostles saw the need to appoint deacons, who were to be helpers in the ministry in such manners as taking care of widows and orphans.

Acts then tells about how not only the apostles went about teaching and sharing Jesus with people, but other disciples were sharing with non-Jews as well. One day, Peter had a vision in which the sky opened up and a sheet filled with various unclean animals was lowered to the ground, and a voice spoke to Peter and said, *"'Arise, Peter, kill and eat.' Peter said, 'By no means, Lord, for these are unclean animals"* (Acts 10:13). The book of Leviticus, part of the Pentateuch, or Torah to the Jews, set out rules for which animals the Jews could eat and which animals were unclean and couldn't be eaten.

The voice came again to Peter and said, "*What God has cleansed, no longer consider unholy*" (Acts 10:15). Peter was perplexed and at the moment did not know what this vision meant. While he was pondering this, some men came to Peter and told them that a certain Roman centurion was asking for him to come up to Caesarea to speak with him. Peter went and the centurion, Cornelius, related to Peter how earlier when he was praying, a man came to him in shining garments. This opened Peter's eyes; for now, he knew what the vision of the unclean animals meant; the gospel of Jesus Christ was meant for all of mankind, not just Jews or the nation of Israel.

The disciples who returned home after the day of Pentecost were also sharing Jesus with the Gentiles in their home areas, many in other countries. Peter felt compelled to report his vision and experience of the centurion with the Christian council in Jerusalem. He was immediately met with disbelief, that the gospel should be shared with the uncircumcised. Peter said that as he was speaking to the centurion, the Holy Spirit fell upon them and even the Gentiles there spoke in tongues.

When the council heard this, they relented and glorified God, saying, "*Well then, God has granted to the Gentiles also the repentance that leads to life*" as He had done with them on the day of Pentecost. He further said, "*If God gave to them the same gift as He gave to us also after believing the Lord Jesus Christ, who are we to stand in God's way*" (Acts 11:17). James, the brother of Jesus, believed by some to be Jesus's cousin had been elected as the head of the church at Jerusalem. He was to be stoned to death on orders of Ananias, the high priest, the same high priest who was responsible for Jesus's crucifixion.

The remainder of the book of Acts deals with the Jerusalem council sending out missionaries to different parts of Asia Minor. The major focus is on Paul's missionary journeys and his establishing of churches throughout what is today Turkey and Greece. He was involved with many different people and dangerous circumstances. He was shipwrecked at one point and placed under arrest on more than one occasion. Even in jail, Paul was given opportunities to witness to people about Christ.

During one imprisonment in Philippi, an earthquake hit the area, and the prison doors were opened. The jailer, fearing that the prisoners had escaped, drew his sword to kill himself. Paul told him not to fear, that all the prisoners were accounted for. The jailer who had been hearing Paul's teachings asked, "*What must I do to be saved?*" Paul responded, "*Believe on the Lord Jesus Christ and thou shalt be saved.*" The jailer took them to his house, and the whole family was saved, and they had a joyful time (Acts 16:30–34).

After Paul returned to Jerusalem from one of his journeys, the high priest, Ananias—yes, the same Ananias that had Jesus arrested and crucified—sought a reason to arrest Paul and on false information had him arrested. The remaining chapters deal with Paul's appearances before the governor and being held for two years, awaiting trial by a succeeding governor. He was able to witness to the governors Felix and Festus, and finally was sent to appear before King Agrippa. Paul told King Agrippa his story of being a devout Jew, even to the point of persecuting Christians; how he was accosted by Jesus on the road to Damascus and became a fervent believer. Paul shared wonderful things about Jesus with the king. King Agrippa listened carefully, and in the end, said, "Almost you have persuaded me to become a Christian." As to the court case, King Agrippa opined that Paul had done nothing worthy of death or imprisonment, and that had Paul not appealed to Caesar, he would have been set free.

So Paul was destined to go to Rome and stand before Caesar to be tried for the charges against him. Perhaps Paul wanted the opportunity to convert Caesar, which would have made Christianity acceptable throughout the Roman Empire. That is only my opinion, but it makes sense.

CHAPTER 15

The Epistles

The next fourteen books after Acts are known as the Epistles, which are the letters that Paul wrote to the churches he had established in Asia Minor and to specific individuals whom he had trained and placed at some of these churches.

Romans

The first Epistle is the letter to the Romans. It is the most instructive of all of Paul's writing regarding how the Christian life is to be lived. The letter to the church in Rome was written from Greece, more specifically when he was in Corinth on his third missionary journey.

The theme of Romans is the same as Peter's vision in Acts, that God offers the gift of salvation to everyone who comes to Jesus by faith. He teaches them that the righteousness that comes from God is not derived from the keeping of the law, but comes by salvation by faith through grace. In chapters 6–8, Paul gives foundational teaching on the spiritual life of a Christian. He describes how to live a balanced life under grace and how to live victoriously through the power of the Holy Spirit. I cannot commend this epistle to you enough. It is foundational to the Christian life.

1 and 2 Corinthians

Paul wrote these epistles to the Christians in Corinth while he was in Ephesus, which was across the Aegean Sea in Turkey. Corinth, being located on the coast, was a large bustling city of world commerce. This was a highly paganistic city so these letters had many teachings against the pagan way of life to the newly converted people. He wrote about factions in the church there, which were barriers to his teachings and to their lives as Christians, as well as lawsuits, immorality, questionable practices, abuse of the Lord's supper, and spiritual gifts. Although Corinth was a Greek city in its location, it had been captured and rebuilt as a Roman colony in 46 BC. One might possibly see how that facilitated distribution of Paul's letters throughout the Roman Empire.

Perhaps the most important and well-known chapter in 1 Corinthians is chapter 13, which is known by Christians worldwide as "the love chapter." Paul describes love as an action, not an emotion. Love is not how we feel toward people, but how we act toward them. He tells the Corinthian Christians to abide faith, hope, and love—these three—but the greatest of these is love.

In 2 Corinthians, Paul addresses a group that has become rebellious of Paul's teaching. They are a minority, but minorities can be very disruptive to the church as a whole. Some of the dissenters were known as Judaizers because they believed that Christians should be circumcised and follow the Mosaic law. Some there also claimed to be apostles and preached a false gospel. He explained that a true apostle is a servant of righteousness and exhibits the characteristics of Jesus Christ, full of love for his fellow man. It isn't the law that saves people, but the grace of God through acceptance of Jesus Christ as Lord.

Galatians

Paul wrote this epistle to the churches in Galatia, of which there were several. Galatia was a geographic region in Asia Minor in what is today Turkey. The Galatians had begun their Christian experience through faith but had somehow gotten offtrack and were now on a course of salvation by works. When we say works, we mean strict obedience to the law or commandments. Paul tells them, again that the believer in

Christ is no longer under the law but grace. We can learn much from this book because it applies to us as well. We are under the law of love. This does not mean that we ignore the law altogether. Faith sets men free to enjoy liberty in Christ. We are free to produce the fruits of righteousness through a spirit-led life. In Galatians 5:22–23, we find that the fruits of the spirit-led life are love, joy, peace, patience, kindness, goodness, faithfulness, gentleness, and self-control. How do we fulfill the law? Love. Love God and your neighbor as yourself.

Ephesians

The books of Ephesians, Philippians, Colossians, and Philemon were written by Paul during his first Rome imprisonment. The book of Ephesians encourages the believer to walk in accordance with his heavenly calling in Christ Jesus. There were no particular problems existing in the church in Ephesus, which has, in part, led to the belief that the letter was more a general letter to Christians in all the churches in Asia Minor.

In the first three chapters of Ephesians, Paul tells the Christians there of the spiritual riches they have inherited as a result of their salvation by grace. They have been adopted by God through their acceptance of Jesus Christ, they have been redeemed through the blood of Jesus, they have been forgiven, and they have been sealed by the Holy Spirit. Then in the last chapters, he tells the Christian to walk in a manner worthy of the calling with which they have been called. How? By being humble, patient, showing forbearance to one another in love.

This is a letter to Christians everywhere, both then in Asia Minor and to us today. Very importantly, in chapter 6, he tells us to put on the armor that God provides us: gird our loins with truth, put on the breastplate of righteousness, take the helmet of salvation and the sword of the Spirit, which is the Word of God. When we are dressed in the armor of God, we will be able to withstand the attempts of the devil to turn us back to our previous sinful self.

The best book I have ever read on Ephesians was probably thirty years ago and is entitled *Sit, Walk, Stand* by Watchman Nee. I commend it to you, if you can find it.

Philippians

While this letter is written as a thank-you to the people of the church of Philippi in Macedonia for the financial assistance they had sent him while imprisoned in Rome, Paul uses it as an occasion to encourage them in Christian unity. Some workers in the church were at odds, which hindered their work in spreading the good news there. Paul writes a little about his imprisonment and how it has actually benefitted the spread of the gospel to the praetorian guard and everyone else he has the occasion to meet. He says, *"For to me, to live is Christ, and to die is gain"* (Philippians 1:21). And he gives us a verse we all can claim, *"I can do all things through Christ who strengthens me"* (Philippians 4:13).

Very important to us is this guidance in Philippians 4:6–8: *"Be anxious for nothing, but in everything by prayer and supplication with thanksgiving let your requests be made known to God. And the peace of God, which surpasses all comprehension, shall guard your hearts and your minds in Christ Jesus. Finally, brethren, whatever is true, whatever is honorable, whatever is right, whatever is pure, whatever is lovely, whatever is of good repute, if there is any excellence and if anything worthy of praise, let your mind dwell on these things."*

Colossians

As in Ephesians, Paul writes initially of the great spiritual benefits of being a Christian, how Christ reconciled them to Himself through his death on the cross for their sins. He tells them that having been raised up with Christ, they are to seek the things above where Christ is seated on the right hand of God; to set their minds on things above, not on things on earth.

Again, this is an epistle to us today as it was to the Colossian Christians. We are to put off the old man with its multitude of sins: immorality, evil desires, greed, malice, slander, etc. We are to put on the new man with a heart of compassion, kindness, humility, gentleness, and patience—bearing with one another, forgiving each other, just as the Lord has forgiven us.

1 and 2 Thessalonians

In Thessalonians, Paul follows the same pattern as in the previous letters by commending the Christians in Thessalonica and then continuing to give them encouragement and instructions for living the Christian life.

Timothy

The letter to Timothy is somewhat different in that it is written to a specific person whom Paul had trained to be a missionary. Timothy is the pastor at the church in Ephesus. Paul sets out the model for bishops, deacons, elders, and teachers—how they are to be above reproach in all their relationships. Timothy is a must read as it tells us the qualifications of leaders in the church.

Hebrews

The book of Hebrews is an epistle written to Jewish Christians, and its author is unknown. However, the author is encouraging those Christians to stay the course and not revert back to Judaism and dependency on the law for salvation. He tells of the superiority of Christ over Moses or any high priests that were in Jewish history. The character of their lives must be shaped by their dedication to Christ and thus will be manifested by their love for each other.

Peter, James, and 1, 2, and 3 John

The epistles of James, 1 and 2 Peter, and 1, 2 and 3 John are similar to the Pauline letters in that they tell us how to live our lives daily as Christians.

James

James wrote his epistle to encourage Christians to be active in serving their fellowman. He says that having faith is only part of a Christian's belief and actions. James 2:24 says, "*You see that a man is justified by works, and not by faith alone.*" You can have faith and tell the needy person to be filled and warmed, but unless you provide him food and clothing, your faith means nothing. We must act out our faith in love.

1 and 2 Peter

The author of these two books is none other than the apostle Peter whom Jesus said He would build His church upon. Peter addressed his first epistle to Christians scattered throughout five provinces of Asia under Roman rule because he had heard they were undergoing persecution by the Roman government. Christians there were relatively new converts, and he wanted to encourage them to live the Christian life of love and serve one another as good stewards of God's grace. He did not want them to give any indication that they were in any way subversive to Rome because of their belief that Jesus was the ruler of "another kingdom." Peter encouraged them to keep fervent in their love for one another because love covers a multitude of sins.

In 2 Peter, he warned Christians about false teachers or opposition from within their group. Having been told that the day of the Lord's return was imminent, some began to grumble and complain about its tardiness. Peter explained the difference in man's thinking on the process of time, saying that to God, one minute is as a thousand years and a thousand years as one minute. Peter cautioned against returning to their pre-Christian ways of carousing, lust, and adultery.

1, 2, and 3 John

The three epistles of John are especially instructive and are written by one who obviously sat at the feet of Jesus while He was on earth and knew firsthand that Jesus was indeed the Son of God. His teachings on love reflect the very words Jesus used when teaching his twelve disciples. John also tells us how we can be sure that we are Christians. *"He that hath the Son hath life, and he that hath not the Son of God hath not life"* (1 John 1:12).

Jude

This final epistle by Jude both encourages Christians and exhorts them to challenge and fight against false teachings that crept into the church, not a specific church, but the church as a whole. Some false teachers have misconstrued the words of Paul that converts are no longer under the law, but under grace. They basically say that gives them license to sin with impunity. This flies in the face of what Jesus said in Matthew 5: 17-20, *"Think not that I am come to destroy the law, or the prophets: I am not come to destroy, but to fulfil it."* In Romans 6: 14, Paul said, "You are not under law but under grace." Paul links the grace of God to the keeping of the law of Christ and the leading of an obedient life.

Who was Jude? Scholars believe that he was the brother of James, the head of the first church in Jerusalem, and also the brother of Jesus.

CHAPTER 16

THE REVELATION TO JOHN

This book is the most complex and difficult book in the Bible. This is the recording of a vision that the apostle John had when he was exiled on the island of Patmos. Ultimately, it reveals the plans of God for the last days for mankind on earth—that is, the days leading up to the return of Jesus Christ to claim His own for eternity. There is so much symbolism that I will not try to explain it. I haven't got it all figured out yet. There are lots of reference books available and always the internet to help you with the symbolisms.

Most instructive are Christ's messages to the seven churches in Asia Minor (present-day Turkey). He reminds each of them of some ways they have departed from their original beliefs, some even to the point of worshipping Balaam. Another church tolerates the woman Jezebel who calls herself a prophetess but is in fact immoral. The messages to the churches are similar to those of the prophets in the time of the kings of

Israel: repent and turn back to being obedient to the Lord, serving one another in love.

The key is that Jesus Christ is coming back for his own. Will you be one of those whose name is in the Lamb's Book of Life?

CHAPTER 17

Making Sense of the Bible

Throughout the Bible, the message is all about the heart of man and what it is focused on. When Samuel was looking for the right man to anoint to become king, he said, "*God does not look on outward appearances. He looks at the heart.*" Proverbs 23:7 says, "*As a man thinks in his heart, so is he.*" When our heart rejects God, He wants us back. Going to church is a good thing, but it is not a requirement. It is a place to worship God with other people as it says in Hebrews 10:25: "*Do not forsake the assembling of yourselves together, but come together to comfort and encourage one another and build up one another in faith.*"

The church of Jesus Christ is not a building; it is the body of Christ. In the book of Jeremiah, we find that the Jews thought "the temple" was the magic word by which they were acceptable to God. Through Jeremiah, God told the people, "*Do not trust in deceptive words, saying, 'The temple of the Lord, the temple of the Lord, the temple of the Lord.' Amend your ways, change your hearts, practice justice between you and your neighbors, do not oppress the widows and orphans."* Micah 6:8 says it so well, *"I have told you, O man, what is good, and what does the Lord require of you, but to do justice, love kindness, and to walk humbly with thy God."*

Now a few words about the Trinity. The term *Trinity* is not in the Bible. It is the name we have given to the three personages of God. God is known as the triune God, consisting of the Father, the Son, and the Holy Spirit. God the Father is the creator of all things, the omniscient, omnipresent Being. He is the God who loves us. God the Son is Jesus, whom God sent to earth in human bodily form to be an example of how we are to live and also to pay the penalty for our sins. The Holy Spirit is the comforter that Jesus promised his disciples when his death was imminent by crucifixion. Jesus said *"When I go, I will leave you with a helper to abide with you. He will be your connection with me and with the Father"* (John 15:26–27, paraphrased).

The Holy Spirit is that still small voice that tells us what is right from wrong. He is our daily companion when we have accepted Jesus as our Savior. If you have not given your heart to Jesus Christ and you are hesitating because you think you have to become a monk, evangelist, missionary, or something else, that is not the case. Accepting Jesus Christ as your Savior simply means confessing to him that you are a sinner, that you are sorry for your sins, and you want the forgiveness that Christ gives to those who humbly ask. It means a change of direction in your life, a new direction and commitment in your heart that you want what God gives: forgiveness, peace, and eternal life. Nothing else. It means you want to live a life pleasing to God in all that you think, say, and do. That's it.

Finally, a word about baptism. When one accepts Jesus as Savior, baptism is not a requirement. Baptism is a ritual that symbolizes to the world that you have undergone a radical change in your life. Being buried in the water indicates the death of the old man and arising from the water is the emergence of a new creature. Baptism is a wonderful experience and demonstrates your conscientiousness in your decision and your faith in God.

Knowing and accepting Jesus is life-changing. You will be happy, have inner peace. People will see the change in you and ask, "What has happened to you? You seem happy, content." Then you can share with them the source of your happiness.

I encourage everyone to begin a systematic reading of the Bible from cover to cover. The more you read it, the more God will reveal its treasures to you. The Word is life. Jesus is the Word. John 3:16 says, *"For God so loved the world that he gave His only begotten Son, that whosoever believes in Him may have eternal life."*

CHAPTER 18

WHAT THE BIBLE IS ALL ABOUT

I hope that this book has helped you understand that the Bible is our handbook for living. It is all about Jesus Christ and salvation through Him: the foretelling of his coming in the Old Testament through the stories of diverse people God selected to accomplish His will, and His arrival in the New Testament giving us the example of how He wants us to live: to love God with all our heart and love our neighbor as we love ourselves. Jesus completes his time on earth by going to the cross to die for yours and my sin. The Bible is all about a loving God who created us and wants to have a personal relationship with us—a God who is there for us even when we leave Him. When we live in Him through Jesus Christ, we live a complete life worth living.

The Bible is God telling us that no matter what we do, He loves us. The most important words in the Bible are the words of Jesus in the New Testament. Jesus's words are the ones we should read and concentrate on when we start out our day. The more we read the Bible, the more its words indwell us and help us to live the Christian life.

May God richly bless you as you take the journey to prayerfully read the Bible through from cover to cover.

ABOUT THE AUTHOR

William has been a Christian since he was a pre-teen and is a retired army officer. He is a graduate of Cottondale (Florida) High School, Chipola Junior College in Marianna, Florida, and Florida State University, and he earned his master's degree from Central Michigan University.

Printed in the USA
CPSIA information can be obtained
at www.ICGtesting.com
LVHW040350290224
772928LV00003B/434